Kind Words About Acoustic Stories

66 **A**lthough his stories are set in a world populated with famous names, his work is emphatically not about name-dropping.

He has created appealing and delightful stories that offer us a slice of the folk music life, and a tasty sampling of the stew of human interaction on stage and off.

He is a gifted wordsmith and a wonderful chronicler of the life he's known; he's giving voice to a culture.

I see parallels in his work and the work of the cowboy poet — both let us see inside a life-style that most of us will otherwise never get to experience.

I don't know anyone else who's doing the work Bill Amatneek's doing: telling funny, sweet, thoughtful, humble, generous stories about the very specific and rarefied culture of the folk musician.

I think the folk music world has found its Homer."

— *Milbre Burch*
National Storytelling Network
Circle of Excellence Storyteller

"Your stories speak to the folk-revival movement, create a bridge to younger generations, and stand alone as pieces of literature."

— *Lisa Null, folklorist, performer*

" 'Paris Remembers' is a great story!"

— *Pete Seeger*

"When I heard you at the *National Storytelling Festival*, you told a story about performing with Peter, Paul & Mary, and it was absolutely entrancing — you struck a chord with everyone in that theater…. I knew that your tremendous talents and truly unique blend of stories would be a wonderful addition to WinterTales. My expectations were fully realized for you moved us all with the power of your telling and the depth of your experience. It was a joy and a pleasure to have the opportunity to work with you — an experience I will hold dear always."

— *Sandy Wright, Director, WinterTales 2000, OKC, OK*

"Bill, this is Ed Enright of *Down Beat* calling. It's Tuesday night. I'm sitting here at home doing a little homework, doing a little editing and stuff, …. Got your piece. 'Jazzbeaux Got There,' read it just this minute, and it is absolutely beautiful, wonderful, unbelievably good. I just wanted to let you know that. This is a piece I'm going to really be proud of putting in the magazine."

— *Ed Enright, Editor, Down Beat*

" 'Layin' Buddy Down' is great material, and a perfect, professional specimen of a personal essay — enough research, detail, and feeling to hold the whole thing in the road from start to finish. Graceful ending, smart structure, nothing missing."

— *Hal Crowther, essayist*

"During my near twenty years at Sweetwater, there were only a small handful of performers whose sheer poignancy made me cry: Watching John Lee Hooker walk on stage; Elizabeth Cotten, at age 88, forgetting the words to her song 'Freight Train,' and the audience singing the lyrics for her; Ralph Stanley singing so lovingly about his departed brother, Carter; Alan Shamblin telling how he came to write 'I Can't Make You Love Me,' which became a huge hit for Bonnie Raitt; and Bill Amatneek, when he finished telling 'Paris Remembers.' It was so touching I burst into tears."

— *Jeanie Patterson, owner, Sweetwater, 1979-1998*
Mill Valley, CA

" 'Jazzbeaux Got There' was just extraordinary. You made the evening for me. People were so touched, applause would have been a violation of the space you had created. That is the highest mark of respect. That closing was the most powerful I've experienced, ... the work of a master."

— *Jim Cooke, director of SSSSSH,*
Second Sunday Seven-Seventeen Story Hour

"Your stories are MUSIC to my ears."

— *Mary Carter Smith, African Griot*

Affiliations are listed for identification purposes only.

Acoustic Stories

For Mike McIntyre —
w/ my thanks
for your beautiful words.

Bill Noailhuck

Acoustic Stories

Bill Amatneek

Vineyards
Press
Sebastopol

Vineyards Press, LLC
P.O. Box 716
Sebastopol California 95473
http://www.VineyardsPress.com

Publisher's Cataloging-in-Publication

Amatneek, Bill
    Acoustic stories : playing bass with Peter, Paul, & Mary, Jerry Garcia, and Bill Monroe, and eighteen other unamplified tales / Bill Amatneek — 1st ed.
    p. cm.
    ISBN 1-928578-11-X
    1. Amatneek, Bill. 2. Folk musicians—United States —Biography. 3. Double bassists—United States— Biography. 4. Popular music—United States—History and criticism. I. Title.

ML419.A57A3 2003   782.42162'0092
Library of Congress Control Number: 2003105666

9 8 7 6 5 4 3 2 1 First Edition - First Printing

Book Design by Bill Amatneek for Vineyards Press, LLC

Printed in the United States of America

To
Ethel & Karl
my favorite mom and dad

Contents

Preface

For most of my life I've played string bass in bluegrass, folk, and big bands. I feel fortunate to have picked with some talented musicians along the way including fiddler and composer Mark O'Connor, singer-songwriter Kate Wolf, and on the first David Grisman Quintet album. Playing music has been a deep pleasure for me, a lifelong blessing of many memorable, transcendent moments.

This is a collection of twenty-one stories about times I've had in music and with musicians. Many started out as stories that I told at SSSSSH (the Marin County story swap group), and at folk, bluegrass, and storytelling festivals.

Storytellers talk about the difference between facts and truth. Facts are what journalists supposedly pursue: the absolute reality. For storytellers, the Grail is truth. By this they mean the fundamental reality of the story, also called the heart. If they have told the heart of the story, then they have told its truth, even if alleged facts have been stretched or ignored.

With most of these stories I told the tale factually, and took time to research the facts and find the photos. Some tales here are told *from* their facts but *to* their hearts. In a very few I have used pseudonyms — had to — or invented particulars. And with a large smile I have most likely added to or spread the legends of a couple legendary musicians, as I believe you will see.

I love playing bass in bluegrass and string bands, but also in jazz big bands. Both these proud forms, bluegrass and big band, are indigenous American musics. And both are fiercly acoustic. Acoustic music fills my senses but never overloads them. Real wood, pure brass, real reeds, skins and hands: wailing or whispered, acoustic music lets my ears all the way in. Given my love of unamplified music, I call these tales "Acoustic Stories."

Friend and master book designer, Pete Masterson, looking over the galleys of this book, said, "Of course, you're using nonstandard typographic conventions." Pete was right. A storyteller's use of rhythm, gesture, expression, sweat, motion and emotion — but most importantly rhythm — are not easily shown with printed words. The nonstandard typographic conventions are my try at restoring some of what is lost as a told tale stretches out on a printed page.

March 25, 2003
Sebastopol, California

Introduction

We lived on Bleecker Street in New York's Greenwich Village in the mid-1940s. I remember sitting around the piano playing down the *Fireside Book of Folk Songs*, mom at the keyboard, dad on mandolin, my sister, me, everyone, singing "On Top of Old Smoky." Dad was an electrical engineer at *Consumer Reports*, so we were the first people on the block to have tape recorders and televisions.

Pete Seeger, the Weavers, Charity Bailey, and other Village musicians came over to have dad record them on one of the first home reel-to-reel tape recorders so they could hear themselves played back. I remember Lee Hays and Pete playing 4-hand piano in our living room.

Mom graduated in piano from the Julliard High School of Performing Arts. She played with deep feeling, loved Chopin, and was an exceptional sight-reader. Paul Robeson would come by. I remember him singing while mom accompanied on the Chickering upright. He sang "No more driver's lash for me," and he spat out the word "lash" like he meant it.

I played violin in the Turtle Bay Music School string ensemble, my first music group. Our debut gig was at Carnegie Hall. We joined kids' string groups from around the city that had been practicing the same material. Together we formed a large youth orchestra that filled the stage and parquet seats.

I remember mom and dad taking me to see Arturo Toscanini conduct. I was very young, three or four, and they told me to be quiet and watch the man who directed the orchestra. He was very old and might die soon. He was brilliant, they said, and I should remember.

We took our seats and I looked around. A thick brass railing surrounded the conductor's podium; I asked my folks why that was.

They said it was because he was old and sometimes he got so excited waving his baton that he had to hold on to the railing to keep from falling. I can still see him conducting, thin face pale as his tux shirt, and I remember closing my eyes and trying to listen hard.

I recall the Weavers' first Carnegie Hall concert in 1955 and the excitement that crackled the air. We got out of the car and rushed towards the hall. Other people were rushing along with us, and I asked my dad, "Poppa, why is everyone so excited?"

"Because Pete and the Weavers are playing a concert."

"But we've been to plenty Weavers' concerts."

"Yes, but not at Carnegie Hall, son. This is their first time at Carnegie Hall."

The roasting coffee aroma of Bleecker Street, pushcart peddlers selling fresh fish, outdoor art festivals with paintings hung on neighborhood fences, the ice creamery where one day the price of a cone went from a nickel to a dime, Pete Carbone's violin store, a forest of dark woods redolent of warm horsehide glue: I recall the old Village, very much an Italian neighborhood, maybe twenty percent boho.

I played cymbals and bass drum in my high school's marching band, and double bass in the orchestra, big band, and with the Philadelphia Folk Workshop. I remember playing bass at the first Philadelphia Folk Festival in 1963 behind the Greenbriar Boys — Ralph Rinzler, Bob Yellin, and John Herald.

And I remember Peter, Paul & Mary.

NOEL PAUL STOOKEY, MARY TRAVERS & PETER YARROW
ACCOMPANIED BY THE AUTHOR
BREAD AND ROSES FESTIVAL OF MUSIC, BERKELEY, OCTOBER 7, 1979

BY JON SIEVERT

MARY, ...

Peter & Paul

Peter, Paul & Mary came to my attention in 1962, when they released their first album, also called, "Peter, Paul & Mary." The two guys in the group, Noel Paul Stookey and Peter Yarrow, both played guitar and sang.

And there was one woman singer, Mary Travers.

She was blond, blue-eyed, with a radiating smile and a chorus of curves. Mary sang sweetly; her harmonies shimmered.

To my eyes, she was beautiful.

I was a seventeen-year-old folk music fanatic when their album came out, and I'll admit, I had a crush on Mary.

So I was delighted when I got a call in 1979 from Mimi Fariña of the Bread and Roses Festival of Music. Peter, Paul & Mary were going to be playing the festival that year and had requested my services as the festival's house bass player to back them for their show. Rehearsal would be the day before the show, backstage, at one o'clock sharp.

They overnighted me their set list, I bought the three Peter, Paul & Mary albums I needed to cover the tunes on the list, and started studying the bass parts.

This is what I found: all of Peter, Paul & Mary's tunes are fairly straightforward, as far as the bass player goes, with one exception, and that's their big hit "Leaving on a Jet Plane." The bass man kicks off this arrangement playing a melodic bass lead. He starts the song off, sets the tempo, sets the groove, and sets the mood of "Leaving on a Jet Plane," playing a bass line that is part melody and part bass vamp.

As the lone bass, new boy on their block, opposite three people who had been playing together for almost a quarter century, when it came to kicking off "Leaving on a Jet Plane," I was scared witless.

Finally the big day of the big rehearsal arrives and I get to the theatre at twelve o'clock, in plenty of time to get real nervous. Then, at one o'clock sharp, in walks MARY ! ...

... and Peter and Paul.

Let me say this: Mary is even more beautiful than her album cover shots show her. Just seeing Mary has got my heart pounding.

She walks right over to me — I stand up immediately — introduces herself, and gives me a hug. YES!

Then she introduces me to Peter and Paul. We shake hands.

The four of us go over to a rehearsal nook back stage, take out our instruments and tune up. By now it is clear that Peter is their MD, their musical director, and Peter calls the first tune for the afternoon:

"Let's try 'Leaving on a Jet Plane' first," he says.

An acid churn hits the pit of my stomach as I realize he's called this tune as a test for me.

Then he turns to me — not Mary and Paul — he turns to *me* and says:

"Ready?"

Well, I know what "Ready?" means. It means, "You do know why I'm calling this tune first, don't you kid?"

I look over at him and say, " 'Leaving on a Jet Plane.' You guys recorded it in the key of A major, but it opens in E major. Peter, ... I'm ready."

Peter counts off "Leaving on a Jet Plane."

"One ... two ... one, two, three, four."

I play the bass part just like I had always practiced.

The three of them look up at me with big, pleased smiles. Mary stands up, walks over to me, looks me right in the eyes, and sings:

> *All my bags are packed, I'm ready to go,*
> *I'm standing here outside your door,*
> *Hate to wake you up to say good-bye.*

Mary, you can wake me up any time.

> *But the dawn is breaking, it's early morn,*
> *Taxi's waiting, he's blowin' his horn,*
> *Already I'm so lonesome I could cry.*

You and me both, Mary.

> *So kiss me and smile for me,*
> *Tell me that you'll wait for me,*
> *Hold me like you'll never let me go.*
> *I'm leaving on a jet plane,*
> *Don't know when I'll be back again.*

Then Mary looks at me longingly, and sings:

> *Oh babe,*
> *I hate to go.*

Well, it is a sweet and deep feeling to be on the bass-bottom of this classic acoustic harmony, surrounded by the singing of the voices who had created it. I know now that Peter,

Paul & Mary mean what they are singing and mean what they are saying. Peter, Paul & Mary *are* who they sing they are.

The rest of the rehearsal goes very well, as does our concert the next evening. It's a funny thing about shows, though. The show itself can go by in a moment. But there are moments in the show that seem to last forever.

I remember one of those moments.

Towards the end of their concert, Paul steps to the center mike to sing the first two verses of a ballad. And Mary ... Mary saunters back to where I'm playing bass. She comes up on my right side, and she puts her hand ... on my shoulder.

Then she rests her head on my arm.

She looks up at me, real slowly.

I look down at Mary.

She looks deep into my eyes.

I look deep into her eyes ....

And then it hits me:

Mary *loves* me. I can tell. Mary loves *me!*

Well, I'm floating. I'm blissed. I don't know how I finish the tune. I don't know how I finish the set. But three tunes later their concert is over, and they leave immediately, ... on a jet plane no less.

I don't even get to say good-bye to Mary.

I don't even get to see her again for a year and a half.

Finally, I read in the paper that they're playing the Circle Star Theatre in San Carlos. So the big night of the big show arrives, and I drive out to see them. I go to the stage door, knock on the door, and who opens it but Mary! She gives me a big hug and a kiss.

But, they're about to go on stage, so I say, "OK babe, I'll see *you* after the show," and I rush to the back of the theatre to watch their concert from there. They put on a terrific show for a receptive, mixed-age crowd; the audience sings along all night. Peter, Paul & Mary are consistently excellent performers. Towards the end of the show, Paul steps to the center mike to sing the same two verses of that same ballad.

And Mary, ... Mary saunters back to where the bass player, Richard Kniss, is playing bass. She comes up on his right side, and she puts her hand ... on *his* shoulder.

Then she rests her head on *his* arm.

She looks up at *him* real slowly.

He looks down at her ...

And that's when it hits me: Mary doesn't love me.

She looks at *all* her bass players that way!

She was using me,

... as a prop,

... ... in her act.

I played a rehearsal, a sound check, a pre-show warm-up, and two shows with them, all in the course of a day and a half. But in that short time I feel I had touched the Peter, Paul & Mary experience, as it surely had touched me.

It was an honor and a thrill to play with them on stage. I must remember to thank them all for it, and to tell Mary ...

> *So kiss me and smile for me,*
> *Tell me that you'll wait for me,*
> *Hold me like you'll never let me go.*

> *I'm leaving on a jet plane,*
> *Don't know when I'll be back again.*

> *Oh babe,*
> *I hate,*
> *to go.*

Mary, ... babe, all is forgiven.

The Philadelphia Folksong Society

Presents

BOB DYLAN

In Concert

Friday, May 3, 8:30 P.M.

Ethical Society Auditorium - 1906 Rittenhouse Sq.

Donation: $1.75 Members: $1.50

TICKETS AVAILABLE:
Gilded Cage, 261 S. 21 St. and at the door

Dylan Plays Philly

Back in 1963, I was a string-bass poppin', banjo-pickin', Philadelphia folkie. The folk scene was small then, and Philly was just a two-hour drive from New York, so what went on in the Apple was known soon and known well in the City of Brotherly Love.

Bob Dylan was what was going on in New York. *Sing Out!* magazine tracked Dylan's rise from early on, and everyone in town was talking about him, though most of us had never seen him.

Back then, the folk music scene had its camps. The bluegrass boys, old-timey folks and traditional balladeers often hung in the same circles. The ragtime fans and blues folks seemed to share an affinity. And certainly the political singers and ethnic music fans seemed to be into their own worlds.

But Dylan, it was said, was none of these.

Dylan, it was said, was something else.

Everyone, in every corner of the Philly folk scene, was looking forward to his first local gig.

. . .

On May 3, 1963, Dylan arrives for his first Philly concert, just weeks before his second album comes out.

> *Some testify that he arrives on his motorcycle, a pre-release copy of his new album tucked under his black leather jacket. His girlfriend Suze rides pillion, her arms wrapped around him like a circle 'round the sun.*
> *And some say that they themselves drive to the 30th Street Station to pick him up. He's alone, no album.*

Dylan's gig is at the Ethical Culture Society hall on Rittenhouse Square in downtown Philadelphia. The seating is 300; that's what the sign over the front door says.

And even at a ticket price of $1.50 for Philadelphia Folksong Society members, and $1.75 for the general public, Bob has that hall filled.

But the 8:30 show time comes and goes, and Dylan has not stepped on stage. Having arrived early, I have a front row seat. There's a door ten feet in front of me that leads backstage. So I decide to see what's happening, where Dylan is. I step through the door, into the Ethical Culture Society's backstage area. There is a hallway leading to the wings, steps going up to the catwalk, and steps leading down. I go down.

After some staircase twists and blind corridors, I see Dylan. There's no manager, no agent, no entourage. Just him, his guitar, and his harmonica. At the moment I set eyes on him, he's backing out of a janitor's closet, having wisely decided that it is not the way to the stage. He looks vibrant and bright-eyed, inner-driven, inner-held ... and lost.

So I say, "Lookin' for the stage, Bob?"

"Yeah."

"Follow me." I lead him up to the stage level and point him to the wings.

As he walks by me to the stage, he says, "Thanks, man."

There were two sets that evening with a good break between, so we all went outside. I remember this: no matter which folk camp you came from, you recognized that what Dylan was doing had not been done before.

First off, no one who wrote songs was also performing them. Sure, Woody Guthrie wrote his own material, but most folks I knew hadn't even seen Woody. Everything Dylan did that evening was his own work, and his work was deeply personal. His lyrics exposed who he was and how he felt, and he felt passionately.

No one sang like Dylan. His shouted vocals, harangued with a nasalized twang, were ear-searing. His midwesternese, now widely copied, had never been heard before. Sometimes he'd squeeze more words into a line than its meter could handle, or put an odd number of lines in a verse, and get away with it poetically.

A harmonica? No one was putting a harmonica on a holder and playing it along with guitar. No one. Most harpists back then played cross-harp style, sucking in on the notes to bluesify them. But Dylan mostly played blow harp. He blew out to play, and the melodies he blew were his own jingle-jangle.

His absorption in each song was mesmerizing, and put you in *to* the Dylan haze. He made no introductions or small talk. He didn't try to charm or entertain. He dove into each song and executed it — tore it up. Dylan was ferocious. A bouncing harmonica, pushed vocals, and a hypnotic guitar accompaniment. He was a three-piece, one-man band.

It seemed as though Bob had questioned the major cornerstones of folk music, from creation through performance, and come back with a new thing.

Sure, there were some pickers who said Dylan was a strummer, not a picker. But his strumming was hammering, and drove his song into you.

There were some singers who said he could not sing. Certainly Bob broke the rules of singing. He'd take a breath in the mid-dle of a word, fergoshsakes. Even folkies knew you didn't do that.

What we all knew was that Dylan had been riveting.

I remember seeing his new album in a record shop window a few weeks later, the cover of him and Suze walking through Greenwich Village snow, her arms yet wrapped around him.

I remember thinking that a sea change was taking place. A new era was beginning: the era of the songwriter as performer, the "singer-songwriter."

After Dylan, whether you were country, folk, R 'n' B, rock, blues or bluegrass, when you walked on stage, you sang your own song.

Mimi Fariña

ANON

Bread and Roses

first heard of her when I was in college. A folkie friend came back from a Boston summer saying that Joan Baez had a younger sister. She was more beautiful than Joan, played guitar better, *and* sang more sweetly. Her name was Mimi.

If true, these were impressive credentials. Joan was gorgeous, an ethereal singer, and a solid guitarist. More beautiful than Joan and a better picker and singer to boot was a combination that was difficult yet pleasing to imagine.

Mimi had married Richard Fariña around then, when she was eighteen. Richard was a novelist, songwriter, and singer who accompanied himself on the dulcimer, a fretted, three-stringed, acoustic instrument. He wrote a novel titled *Been Down So Long It Looks Like Up To Me*. They were living near Carmel when it was published, and went to Richard's first book signing together on April 30, 1966. When it was over, Richard asked an acquaintance for a ride on his motorcycle. He handed Mimi his wallet before he mounted the bike.

Somewhere along the highway they took a bad turn and went off the road. Richard died at the scene, his head against a stone.

Back at a friend's home, waiting with others for Richard's return, Mimi heard sirens and felt something was wrong. They drove down the highway to a crash site where police met them. An officer told them that the driver of a motorcycle had lived but not his passenger. They couldn't identify the victim because he didn't have a wallet. Mimi was holding the wallet in her hand. It was her twenty-first birthday.

In 1974, Mimi started a nonprofit organization in Mill Valley that she called Bread and Roses.

B&R brings free live music to people in Bay Area institutions. They have over a thousand volunteer performers who bring their art to convalescent homes, hospitals, AIDS facilities, homeless and senior centers, psychiatric, rehabilitation and detention facilities, and shelters for runaway kids and homeless people. With over 500 institutional shows a year, they bring entertainment, as Father Guido Sarducci quipped, "everywhere that Jello is served."

Mimi named her organization after the poem, "Bread and Roses," by James Oppenheim. It is said that he wrote it after witnessing a textile strike in 1912, Lawrence, Massachusetts. The women picketers carried signs that sloganized "We want Bread and Roses too." Mimi set the poem to music in 1976 and recorded it with her sister Joan.

As we go marching, marching
In the beauty of the day,
A million darkened kitchens,
A thousand mill lofts gray,
Are touched with all the radiance
That a sudden sun discloses,

For the people hear us singing:
"Bread and Roses! Bread and Roses!"

As we go marching, marching,
We battle too for men,
For they are women's children,
And we mother them again.
Our lives shall not be sweated
From birth until life closes;
Hearts starve as well as bodies;
Give us bread, but give us roses!

As we go marching, marching,
Unnumbered women dead,
Go crying through our singing
Their ancient call for bread.
Small art and love and beauty
Their drudging spirits knew.
Yes, it is bread we fight for —
But we fight for roses, too!

As we go marching, marching,
We bring the greater days.
The rising of the women means
The rising of the race.
No more the drudge and idler
Ten that toil where one reposes,
But a sharing of life's glories:
Bread and roses! Bread and roses!

Our lives shall not be sweated
From birth until life closes;
Hearts starve as well as bodies;
Bread and roses, bread and roses.

. . .

I walked into the Bread and Roses office in 1979, a few months before they mounted their music festival at Berkeley's Greek Theater. I volunteered to be the house string bassist for whomever might ask for my services. They mulled it over and finally said Sure.

A week later Mimi gave me a call. Peter, Paul & Mary had accepted Bread and Roses' invitation to play the festival that year, and had asked for my house-bass-player services. The trio overnighted me their set list, and the rest is a story you've heard. In the two years I played the festival, I had the honor of accompanying the Chambers Brothers, David Bromberg, Jeff Hanna, Paul Siebel, Jethro Burns, Odetta and Tim Hardin, Steve Goodman, and many others.

Some time after that first festival, I started playing behind Mimi in her backup band, joining Lowell Levinger, AKA "Banana," who played banjo, guitar, and piano. We played venues in Northern California and opened for Gordon Lightfoot on a tour of Alaska and Hawaii. The tour started at a high school in Anchorage. We were slated to fly out to Waikiki that night, right after the gig.

So, we're on stage in Anchorage. It's colder than, well ... than Alaska, and Mimi, Banana and I have done our first two tunes. Mimi is into her between-tune patter, and she says,

"Tonight, after playing here for you, we're getting on a plane and flying to Hawaii for our next show." Here she thumbs her nose at the crowd and goes, "Nyah, nyaha, nyah, nyah."

And inside I'm thinking, Holy Toledo, what a risk! These are Alaskans. They love Alaska; they love the cold. This could backfire on her. We could get booed off the stage.

But no, the room bursts into laughter and then applause.

.   .   .

Mimi had pulled off a delightful coup. I appreciate spontaneity in a leader on stage. It can be risky, but when it works you put the entire room on your side. Mimi had the crowd in her hands the rest of the evening.

We played together for a while longer, and co-wrote a song in 1980, "Feeling Left Behind." But after a time, Mimi gave up performing to focus her energies on Bread and Roses.

We both lived in Mill Valley, so we ran into each other occasionally and chatted. When I had my first storytelling gig at Sweetwater, Mimi showed up before the show and gave me a long-stem rose and a note of best wishes. I was deeply touched by her kindness and thoughtfulness.

In November of 1999, Mimi was diagnosed with lung cancer. The news was a shock to all who knew her. She started chemo and radiation treatments that of course led to hair loss. I went to the show that Bread and Roses mounted at the San Francisco War Memorial Opera House on March 20, 2000, celebrating their 25th anniversary. It was a magnificent evening culminating in Pete Seeger singing for the packed house. Mimi was a delightful, entertaining MC, and included some kidding about her losing hair. I sent her a letter a few days later:

> Dear Mimi -
> I just wanted to say congratulations on a wonderful show Monday evening. It was a great concert with some of my favorite entertainers, including your sister, Jackson Browne, Kris Kristofferson, Boz Scaggs, Robin Williams, and Pete. You were an excellent mistress of ceremonies, and you looked gorgeous. It was Boz who said "25 more years," but I believe Bread and Roses will go on for as long as there are prisons and old folks' homes that need entertainment: that is, forever.

I was in Oklahoma City recently, playing their storytelling festival. I mentioned Bread and Roses in the tale I told about playing with Peter, Paul & Mary. After the show, someone in the audience approached me and said that they had started a similar nonprofit in OKC, based on B&R. Of course you know that your organization has inspired and spawned many others. But there it was, looking me right in the face. So, congratulations on Bread and Roses. Congratulations on all its offshoots. But most of all, congratulations and thank you for all the happiness you have brought to everyone in every institution that you have served.

I was more than blown away to hear of your health problems. When we ran into each other recently, you looked great, with hair and all. I think I even mentioned how wonderful you looked.

I could not believe my ears. This must have come up suddenly.

But the big C is no longer the life-defying illness it once was. I believe that the people who beat it are people with purpose, with stamina, and who have a strong support group. Mimi, you have all of these in spades. Please know that you will beat this, that you will live on, healthfully, and that you are by far too high-energy not to survive this battle. Keep your faith, and those of us who know you will keep it with you. May you be blessed with a full recovery.

Best wishes,

Bill Amatneek

A few months later she sent me a note. It was the first cor-respondence I had received from her, and I hung onto it. I have since learned that her notes are treasured by the stars and cons alike who have received them.
    She wrote:

Bill,
Thank you so much for the healing card you sent me. I opened it with joy, with a song in my heart. To be surrounded by friends like you with feelings of love is indeed a blessing. If affects me deeply.
With love to you and for you,

Mimi
P.S. You wrote such a lovely letter. It was more than a card and I appreciate it so. I'm fighting the good fight – be well and take care.

It was the last I heard from her. Mimi passed on July 18, 2001. There was a memorial service for her at San Francisco's Grace Cathedral on August 7. It was a fitting remembrance of and tribute to her life, and a turning point for me.

Mimi was eulogized by a number of folks, none more touchingly than her mother, Big Joan, or more insightfully than her sister, Joan. I think with deaths such as Mimi's — those that are a while in coming — that people have time to adjust some to the situation. Sudden deaths throw people; the memorial that follows hears the wailing that accompanies abrupt departures. But the eulogizers at Mimi's memorial were remarkably dry-eyed in their memories of Mimi and insights into her life.

Grace Cathedral is resonant and vibration-filled. Between speakers there was time to reflect, so I closed my eyes and tried to come to terms with my relationship with Mimi. What did I have to learn from it?

Mimi had created a few folk "hits" in her day, some with Joan, some with Richard, some with Tom Jans later on, and some on her own. Her best-known song, written by Richard and Pauline Marden, and recorded by Mimi and Richard, is called "Pack Up Your Sorrows."

The melody of the chorus, as well as the song's sentiment, are charming and memorable. Although other folks recorded this piece subsequently, Mimi's rendition is the one most people remember.

She penned another tune called "In the Quiet Morning," an elegy for Janis Joplin that to my ears demonstrates deft song-writing skills. Both of these tunes are recognizable to anyone who was around the folk music movement when they were released. There were other tunes that Mimi wrote, co-wrote or recorded that became well-known in the folk music community.

Mimi had a story that was being told by the time she was a teenager. Her story had gained the stature of legend by the time Richard died. Just the tale that I heard about her from my college friend — that she was younger, prettier, played better and sang sweeter than Joan — was legend material.

Mimi came, I believe it is fair to say, from a family whose politics were progressive. So did I. When you have this background, you learn that you have two obligations.

The first is to help your fellow man, especially the less rich, the less educated, the newer to these American shores, … the less well-off. The second is to leave this world a better place than when you entered.

Mimi took these lessons to heart; she dedicated her life to these tenets with Bread and Roses. B&R has done many thousands of gigs for people who were uplifted by the experience. In that, Mimi helped humankind immeasurably *and* left this world better off.

Listening to everyone who eulogized her — Reverend Alan Jones, John Burton, Lana Severn, Cassandra Flipper, Paul Liberatore, her sister, and her mother — I heard that it was Bread and Roses, and not Mimi's music, which would define her life. I realized how hard she had worked on it, how it would outshine and outlast her music contributions.

I saw that my one objection to Bread and Roses — that Mimi and her staff were paying themselves to administer the organization, but that the performers were not being paid for their work — was part of the formula, of the formula's magic. I saw that for the performers this was the full expression of giving: you gave all you had and received nothing material in return, ... nothing but love. This was what made performing for Bread and Roses the meaningful experience that it was for everyone who played institutional shows for them.

Hearing all this at Grace Cathedral, I started to question my level of participation in society's causes. I had felt stung by my social activism when I was in high school. I had done benefits for a number of needy groups while I was still a teenager, playing banjo, singing, just as I played bass for Bread & Roses many years later.

One summer, following my senior year in high school, I took a day gig with a government-funded research center. In the fall, when I'd gone to college, they sent me a letter. They had heard about these benefits that I had played in my past. They wanted me to tell them about them, and on the basis of what I said, they either would or wouldn't hire me again. A lawyer friend advised me on how to answer their letter, but said that no matter how I responded, I'd never work for the research center again.

It left a bad taste in my mouth about playing for causes. I started feeling ambivalent about performing benefits.

Sitting there in Grace Cathedral that day, listening to what Mimi had done with Bread and Roses, I had to ask myself: what had I been doing to make this world better, to help mankind?

There was only one activity I could possibly point to, and that was playing music. I *hope* it is fair to say that most everywhere I have played, most everyone has walked out feeling better than when they walked in.

But helped the world ... benefitted mankind? I left Grace Cathedral feeling I hadn't done much about that recently.

Two weeks later, Joe Armstrong called me. He asked if I would tell some stories at a benefit for disadvantaged kids in Northern Sonoma County. I told him to sign me up.

Playing bass for the Bread and Roses music festivals was a rich experience, and the story about playing with Peter, Paul & Mary has become an audience favorite. Touring Hawaii, opening for Gordon, and driving home from our Santa Cruz gigs at two in the morning, were all delicious times.

But the lesson learned sitting in Grace, Mimi, is one I will remember.

Dionne Sings

For most folks, the twenty-first birthday is a fairly important one. You probably remember what you did that day, if you're over twenty-one. If you're under twenty-one and you remember your twenty-first birthday, well, you'll have to sort that one out yourself. My twenty-first trip around the sun was in the 1960s, so I would have no memory of it at all were it not for Dionne Warwick.

I was an undergraduate at Penn State University in State College, Pennsylvania, and treasurer of "the world's largest jazz club," as we were fond of boasting, with thousands of paying members.

How did we get that membership? Every spring the club's board of directors would convene and decide on the acts that we would hire for the following fall's concerts. We'd try to book two headliners on the popular side of jazz who could pull a mainstream crowd and fill the 7,500-seat rec hall.

We'd have folks like jazz flutist Herbie Mann. Mann singled on the charts in 1961 with "Comin' Home, Baby." We had Ramsey Lewis one year. Jazz pianist Lewis had a crossover hit in 1965 with "The In-Crowd." We also had Dave Brubeck, with Paul Desmond on sax, Joe Morello on drums, and Ray Brown playing bass. Brubeck was the first jazz artist of his day to appeal to a broader audience, and succeeded wildly with a piece written in 5/4 time called "Take Five."

The revenues from these shows enabled us to have many other, harder-core jazz and blues artists for concerts that were not always profitable. Over the years we hosted: Muddy Waters; Thelonius Monk; John Coltrane; Cannonball Adderly with his brother, Nat Adderly, and saxist Charles Lloyd; Archie Shepp; Horace Silver with Wayne Shorter; Mose Allison with melody drummer Paul Motian; Andrew Hill; and Bill Evans with bassist Eddie Gomez and drummer Marty Morrell. The jazz club was always profitable. At one point we had accumulated so much cash that at my urging we started giving it away to needy causes such as the Committee to Rescue Italian Art, shortly after Florence and Venice experienced catastrophic flooding in 1966.

On the opening day of spring semester, when the student body trooped into the gym to sign up for clubs and activities, the jazz club would have a booth. We'd sell tickets to the headliner concerts we had booked and we'd sell membership in the club. This was the deal: If you bought membership in the jazz club, you got a reduction in ticket price. The reduction was so substantial that if you were buying only two tickets to one show, it was cheaper to pay for membership and get the two reduced-priced tickets than it was to buy two regular-priced tickets without membership. This was the original no-brainer. Even the jocks got it.

On my 21st birthday, in October of 1966, Dionne Warwick came to sing.

Dionne's show was sold out. She was hugely popular in the '60s with hits that were written by Burt Bacharach and Hal David. These were lushly melodic and haunting tunes. There was "I Say a Little Prayer," maybe her best-known recording from that era. Dionne charted with "This Girl's in

Love with You," and "Take a Message to Michael." Everyone remembers "Walk on By." Warwick's sateen voice was the perfect foil for the luscious Bacharach-David compositions. The three produced some long-memorable music.

. . .

I awoke on my birthday and was hardly aware that it *was* my birthday. The day of a major show is busy for folks involved in producing it. Everyone on the board was running around, and I didn't go to a single class, as I recall. But I also recall, as the day wore on, that neither mom, dad, nor my sister had phoned in to sing "Happy Birthday," a longtime family tradition and something they all usually do before noon.

The show that evening was a wild success. Dionne's band was tight and her singing was silken. She had superb communication with the crowd and sang every song we wanted to hear. By the time the show was over, only one person, my girlfriend Susan, bless her heart, had said happy birthday to me all day.

After our concerts, the jazz club's board of directors would put on a party back at our apartment. We'd always invite the artists to join us. If you were a single musician staying overnight in State College following your gig, there was not a lot going on, so you might fall by and take a chance on a party with unknown college kids. And if you weren't in that position, well, probably not.

We approached Dionne after the show and invited her to the party. Dionne was with her mom and it was around midnight. She is a regal and classy lady, and we didn't believe she would be interested in partying with us hippie jazz-club college students ... but she was.

So we all went over to our place — a dozen folks were already there when we arrived — and commenced having a fine old time. Dionne was sociable, chatty, and supremely relaxed after her concert. This was remarkable in itself. Putting on a two-set show to a large crowd is exhausting, physically and emotionally. You get back energy from the crowd. It's not the kind that will set you on a ten-mile jog, but it will keep you awake for at least two hours.

Dionne was more than awake. Her effervescence and relaxed poise, at that time of night and following a large show, was impressive. She was warm, gracious, and engaging.

At a little after midnight, I was standing in the living room talking with Dionne and her mom, and I saw the president of the jazz club, Stan Lathan, bringing a cake with birthday candles out of the kitchen. And I thought, "Well, that's nice. I wonder whose birthday it is? Because it sure isn't mine anymore."

And as he was bringing the cake over, Dionne started singing "Happy Birthday" ... to *me!*

She led everyone in singing happy birthday to me!

That was Dionne and me. Me and Dionne!

Cake. Dionne. Me. Dionne. Candles. Dionne singing, everyone singing "Happy Birthday." To me ... with Dionne.

It was a shimmering slice of twenty-first-birthday heaven.

At about two in the morning, Dionne was sitting next to me and I was sitting next to the phone. She turned to me and said, "Bill, we'd like to go home now. Would you please call us an airplane?"

I'd never been asked to call anyone an airplane, or to call an airplane for anyone. But in a moment I went from thinking, She must be joking, to knowing, She's not.

So I said, "Sure, Dionne," picked up the local yellow pages and started looking under "A" for "Airplane."

Please understand that State College was a small town back then, with one tiny airport. The airport was so small that if a pilot was going to do a night landing, he had to radio ahead to the tower so they could run out and fire up the Tiki torches that lined the dirt runway.

Finally I found an air charter service, although I could tell by the mini-listing that it was a one-man shop: a single guy with a single-engine, four-seat Cessna, trying to make a buck. It was Saturday night, two in the morning, and I called the number. After eight rings a sleepy voice picked up. I asked him if he could fly two people to Philadelphia.

He asked me to hang on, he'd get his appointment book.

I said, "They'd like to leave in twenty minutes."

He said, OK, that he was actually free then.

"How much?" I asked.

"A hundred dollars."

I turned to Dionne and told her that he wanted one hundred dollars — at that time the price of a first class, round trip ticket to Paris — and she said, "Fine." So we bundled up into the car and drove Dionne and her mom to the airport. Sure enough, someone had gone out and lit the Tiki torches. The airplane was tiny, and the pilot looked funny sitting at the controls in his pajamas and bathrobe, but we understood.

Dionne's mom got into the plane, and then Dionne. As I said good-bye to them — I was about to close the door — Dionne waved to me and called out "Happy birthday, Bill!" over the engine's drone.

So Dionne, although other events from the '60s have slipped my mind, this one has not. Thank you so much for a memorable, glistening, twenty-first birthday.

I don't believe I've had "Happy Birthday" sung to me so sweetly since.

FRANK WAKEFIELD
STEVE SWAN GUITARS, KENSINGTON, NOVEMBER 16, 1997

Jesus Loves
His Mandolin Player

I can still remember the first time I heard him play, thirty-five years ago. His music physically hit me as I turned the corner to the theatre. The sound of his mandolin rang out against the red brick walls, hopped over some New England poplars, bounded up the streets of Providence, and stuck right in my ears.

His sound cut. It was woody, it was raw, and even a block away it was blazingly bright.

My ears popped. I was an avid, 22-year-old bluegrass banjo picker and I had come just to hear him play. I chased his sound 'round the side of the theatre and found him outside the stage door leading his band.

His scraggly blond hair framed a ruddy and well-traveled face. He was bent over his mandolin, pickin' and *gleefully* grinnin'. This was Frank Wakefield, hellacious and notorious mandolinist.

His band was rehearsing one last tune, "Blackberry Blossom," before going on stage. Frank's group was tight, though I realized I played banjo a lick or two better than his banjoist.

I didn't say anything of course; I just stood there, smiling broadly, enjoying the music.

They came to the end of the tune, and Frank's banjo man made a big mistake: he put his instrument down and wandered off to find the bathroom. I asked Frank if I could play a tune with him on the kid's banjo, and he said, "Sure, go ahead."

Frank's playing soared. Standing there pickin' with him, I realized that this was the first time I had played with anyone who had music in his veins. Frank was burning up with music. Melodies overflowed the *f*-holes of his old Gibson mandolin.

By the time the tune ended, Frank knew that I cut his banjoist. When the guy came back from the bathroom, Frank fired him on the spot ... and then browbeat him into letting me borrow his banjo to play the concert. I rehearsed one more tune with Wakefield's group, and then they called us to go on stage.

As we walked to the wings to be brought on, Frank asked me what I did and if I would like to go on the road with his band. I told him I was staying in Brown University graduate school to beat the Viet Nam draft, but playing with him sure beat that.

We shook on it.

In that moment I quit one graduate school and started another, got my first professional music job, walked on stage to play a sold-out concert with a musical fireball, and oh yes, exposed myself to the wartime, Viet Nam draft.

That afternoon on stage, Frank taught me a lot.

A bluegrass group's performance involves a stylized choreography with its roots in live performance and radio. With only one microphone for the band, players have to map out their stage moves in advance.

You don't want to be stepping up to the mike to sing a verse at the same time the banjoist is swooping in, peghead first, to take a solo. You could get hurt.

But we didn't have time to rehearse the tunes or the moves. During the show Frank hovered in the back of the group and gestured me in and out of the lineup as my entrances came. Before each tune ended he would lean over and tell me the name of the next tune and the key it was in.

When the tune was done and the applause had died, he'd turn to the audience and say something like:

"Thank ya s'much. Y'all make us feel so good when you give us a good hand like that, I swear ya do. And now we'd like to sign up for one that we're gonna put a hurtin' on. We call it 'John Hardy.' "

BAM! I had to nail my introduction as he said "Hardy," in the right key and tempo. On stage that day, Frank showed me that this was what he expected of me.

After the third song, Frank introduced his band to the audience. When he came to me he said: "And on the five-string banjo we got an ol' boy who's gonna be pickin' with me til our men come home from Viet Nam, cause that's the only way he's a gonna beat the draft. But why don'tcha make him welcome anyway ... Bill Matnick."

What was that? It didn't matter. The flush of a hot spotlight hitting me and the crowd cheering felt terrific.

The audience ate us up and brought us back for an encore. Frank decided on the Bill Monroe mandolin instrumental, "Rawhide."

Everyone takes a solo on "Rawhide." So, my turn comes, I play my solo, and I'm putting the last four bars on it, when I feel Frank come up behind me. As my chorus ends, he pushes my left hand off the banjo neck. I can't play with that hand now! And Frank starts fretting my banjo with his left hand while I am still picking the strings with my right.

It works! The crowd breaks into applause. They've never seen anything like this.

FRANK-PICKIN'

BY GENE TORTORA

I've never seen anything like this, and I'm doing it.

But it ain't over. Still fretting my banjo and strumming his mandolin, Frank maneuvers his instrument so it is within my reach. And he gestures for me to play his mandolin with my left hand.

Mind you, Frank doesn't know if I play mandolin or not. He's relying on the bluegrass tradition that every picker picks a little on the three fretted instruments: guitar, banjo and mandolin. Fortunately, Frank is right. My dad is a mandolin player and there have been mandolins in my house all my life. So I reach under Frank's mandolin, grab the neck with my left hand and start fretting the notes that Frank is picking. This locks us in a schizophrenic embrace that splits me in half: I'm a banjo man on one side of me and a mandolinist on the other. Frank has taken me to a place I have never been before.

As we hit the first beat of the last sixteen bars, Frank

pulls one more surprise. He kicks the tune up into double-time tempo, hell-bent for leather. We race to the ending, harmonize on shaves and haircuts, and end the tune with a chop that explodes the crowd.

We exit to thunderous cadence clapping and two-fisted whistling, ... a thrilling concert.

I went on the road with Frank's band for about a year. We played East Coast coffeehouses, college concerts and folk music clubs. In New York, we headlined at Gerde's Folk City for a week; Emmylou Harris opened for us. As I got to know him better, I saw why Frank himself is as legendary as his mandolin playing. He is well-known for a kind of talking, "Frank-talk," which relies heavily on double negatives, non-sequiturs, and plain ol' nonsense.

For instance, I might pick up the phone one day and hear Frank on the other end saying, "Good-bye Frank, this is Bill speakin'. Let's not have dinner with Smoke Dawson tonight at the Cafe Lena. Hello?"

I respond with, "Good-bye Bill, this is Frank speakin'. OK, let's not have dinner with Smoke at the cafe Lena tonight, say 8:00 o'clock. ... Hello?"

Frank can also twist the facts about an event until his telling of it may be somewhat at odds with reality. Here is an example.

There is a well-known story about Frank and his price-less, 1923 Gibson, Lloyd Loar-signed mandolin. At a recording session many years ago, Frank, frustrated over how the work was going, allegedly threw his mandolin to the floor ... hard.

It must have been electrifying to have been there. Acoustic musicians coddle their instruments, clean them after each playing, and even talk to them. Throwing an axe is unheard of, and speaks to just how broken up Frank must have been about the session.

WAKEFIELD REVEALED
FREIGHT & SALVAGE, BERKELEY, NOVEMBER 18, 1997

But the producer just bent down, picked up the instrument, which miraculously had landed undamaged, and handed it back to a chin-on-his-chest Frank.

Recently, I saw Frank and this very producer together, and I heard Frank say to the guy: "You remember that time I was at your house and you threwed your guitar down the staircase?"

Well, this is just Frank talking "Frank-talk."

As I told Wakefield the first time I met him, I was in Brown University's graduate school with a student deferment. Joining his band ended that. I was draft-eligible the entire year I played with him. (A week after I left Frank's group to discover California, Uncle Sam sent me a notice to come in for my physical exam, which I flunked.)

But Frank, who I reckoned was pro-war, got it in his head from our first talk that I had joined his group to evade the draft.

Frank had it that right up there on the government's list of bona fide, draft-deferrable gigs, along with Napalm Bomb Design, was "Picking Banjo In Frank Wakefield's Group." It was such an outlandish claim that I never tried to straighten him out on it. I was Frank's draft-dodger banjo-picker from that first concert until I left his group.

I will admit that sometimes his ribbing got to me.

In the thirty-five years since, I've rarely seen Frank Wakefield; he usually lives East Coast and I live West. But in 1991 he came to play Mill Valley's own Sweetwater, an internationally renowned nightclub, Mill Valleyians want you to know.

Now it may seem to you that Frank is in his own little corner of the music world; the mandolin tunes he has written are uniquely his. Fiercely bluegrass at their heart, some have also been called "classical." His tunes can stop, ... and start up again on an offbeat. This is called "turning the beat around," and is usually avoided; Frank purposely embraces it. Some of his compositions can change time signature for a few measures and then go back to the original time. This too is a tad unusual for bluegrass.

He wrote a song cycle he called "Jesus Loves His Mandolin Player," and surely He must, Frank, because some of those tunes, creatively speaking, and I mean this in the highest complimentary sense, are from somewhere else.

A number of rock and pop stars were brought up on bluegrass and have a direct connection to Frank. In the house that night were Maria Muldaur, who famously sang "Midnight on the Oasis," David Grisman, Wavy Gravy, and David Nelson of the Jerry Garcia Band, and New Riders of the Purple Sage. All have performed with Frank at some time, as have Emmy Lou Harris and Linda Ronstadt, by the way.

There were two sets that night. In the first, Frank played a number of mandolin instrumentals. Some were classics by Bill Monroe, the father of Bluegrass music, and some, like, "New Camptown Races," were classics by Frank. Wakefield lifted the crowd out of their seats and got them dancing in the aisles. The applause was deafening as the band exited the stage; the set was a tribute to Frank's power with his mandolin.

Downstairs during the break, Maria Muldaur rehearsed an old-timey song with Frank, his group, and me sitting in on string bass. It was written by Rosa Lee Watson, Doc Watson's wife, and is called "Your Long Journey."

Maria related that the song came to Rosa Lee one day as she was cleaning house. The thought struck her as to what would happen if her husband Doc was called to heaven before she was.

One of the most haunting songs in the American old-time repertoire, "Your Long Journey," usually sung as a male-female duet, goes like this:

God's given us years of happiness here,
Now we must part.
And as the angels come and call for you,
The pangs of grief tug at my heart.

Oh my darling,
My darling,
My heart breaks as you take
Your Long Journey.

Oh the days will be empty the nights so long
Without you my love.
And as God calls for you I'm left alone,
But we will meet in heaven above.

Oh my darling,
My darling,
My heart breaks as you take
Your Long Journey.

Fond memories I'll keep of happy ways
That on earth we trod.
And when I come we will walk hand in hand
As one in heaven in the family of God.

Oh my darling,
My darling,
My heart breaks as you take
Your long journey.

When the last note of the tune had died, the greenroom went silent. Finally someone said: "What an incredible song."

And someone else echoed, "Amen."

Then it was time for the last set at Sweetwater. I gave Frank a big hug and thanked him for all he had taught me: burning artistry, spontaneity, fiery performance, and a few licks on the 5-string to boot.

We had just started up the stairs — he was carrying his mandolin; I was two steps behind him toting my bass — when he turned around to me and said:

"Ya see. It was good that ya played with my band all them years and stayed out of the draft until the war was over."

I couldn't believe that after all this time, Frank was going to get on about Viet Nam again. I warily looked up at him and asked, "Oh really, Frank? Tell me, why is that?"

Frank told me. He said, "Well, ya didn't go die in some goldern war. And now you're here with us tonight to play beautiful music."

ARETHA FRANKLIN
MAGENTA SUITE, FAIRMONT HOTEL, SAN FRANCISCO, FEBRUARY 1971

BY ANNIE LEIBOVITZ

Aretha Speaks

There are some people in California who are so deeply into astrology, they can tell your sign by the shape of your face. They *know* that Johnny Carson is a Libra, because Johnny Carson's face has that "Libra" shape.

Well, I just don't see it.

And then I met Aretha Franklin.

I was free-lancing for Rolling Stone in 1971 when I heard that Aretha was coming to play the Fillmore Auditorium. I asked my boss, Jon Carroll, if I could interview her for the magazine.

Aretha defined the soul sound of that era with hits such as "Respect," and chain, chain "Chain of Fools." There was the wailing "Dr. Feelgood" in the morning, and the women's anthem, "Do Right Woman," among many others.

Jon laughed at my request. He told me that Aretha was said to be a tough interview; it was not easy to get her to open up. Rumor had it that she felt mistreated by a 1968 cover story in a major weekly magazine, and she was talking to the press even less than usual.

That didn't bother me; I idolized Aretha and asked Jon to set it up.

He set it up.

Jon sent the renowned photographer Annie Leibovitz to do the shoot. I was certainly glad he was sending a pro like Annie, because standing there outside the Magenta Suite of the Fairmont Hotel where Aretha was staying during her gig, my knees were literally shaking.

But I had done my homework. I had chased down a dozen Aretha Franklin albums, listened to them carefully and drawn up a list of questions to ask her: questions about her recordings, her music, ... her life, in a well-prepared, two-hour interview.

Annie and I knocked and were let in by someone who was probably hired to do just that. Immediately, our eyes were assaulted by magenta everywhere we looked. Rugs, walls, furniture ... everything was a shade and design of magenta.

And there was Aretha, seated in a magenta lounge chair, surrounded by an entourage of twenty people. I had never seen an entourage before, but as soon as I saw this group of people hanging on Aretha's every word, I knew: *this* was an entourage.

Annie and I made our introductions and while she started clicking away furiously, I got out my notebook, switched on the tape recorder, and started to interview Aretha Franklin, the Queen of Soul.

Whatever my boss had said about Aretha was wrong. She was not a tough interview; for me, she was impossible.

I asked easy questions, like, "How are you enjoying San Francisco?" and she said:

" ... Good."

I asked open-ended questions, like "Tell me about your six years of recording at Columbia Records," and Aretha said:

" ... Good."

The only thing she wanted to talk about was her soon-to-be-released album, *Young, Gifted and Black*. This was the only album Aretha had made in the last decade that I hadn't been able to get a hold of. Sure, it hadn't been released yet. I went through my list of questions in seven minutes flat. Each elicited a one-sentence answer, max. Annie tried to help me out, she was a sweetheart, but I never got the momentum going with Aretha.

I closed my notebook, turned off the tape recorder, and stood up, indicating the interview was over. Instantly, Aretha dropped her guard and started talking nonstop about the sight-seeing and shopping she'd been doing in San Francisco. Since the entourage was glued to her every word, the room soon got into a group discussion, and the topic moved to astrology.

Then, as we did in those heady days of the early '70s, everyone started asking everyone else, "What's your sign? ... What's *your* sign?"

Aretha turned to me. She said: "I know what your sign is, Bill."

The room went dead. For the first time since we had arrived, Annie put her camera down.

I smiled. It takes most people twelve tries to hit that I'm a Libra. I was sure she didn't have a clue.

"What sign am I, Aretha?"

"Bill, you're a Libra."

"Aretha, no one ever gets that! How could you tell?"

"By the shape of your face."

"The shape of my face!"

"Why yes," Aretha said. "It's just like Johnny Carson's."

TONY RICE
MCNEAR'S THEATRE, PETALUMA, FEBRUARY 21, 1999

TEE

I remember the first time I picked with guitarist Tony Rice. The David Grisman Quintet's first gig, on January 31st, 1976, was in Bolinas, California, where I was living. At that show, Tony was on guitar, Todd Phillips played second mandolin to David's first, Darol Anger played fiddle and Joe Carroll was their bassist. Joe (may he rest in peace) was an excellent bassist — he recorded with Mose Allison, among others — but to my ears his roots were more in jazz than were the group's roots.

Listening to his playing, I said to myself: I can do that. So I tracked down Darol's phone number and hired him to play a square dance gig with me.

After the gig Darol said, "Hey man, I've gotta get you together with Dawg and us. I'll call you." ("Dawg" is David's nickname.)

A few months later the call came, and I drove over to the home David and Janis Bain rented on the shoulder of Mt. Tamalpais. On a warm afternoon, Tony, Darol, Todd, David, and I went into a basement room that overlooked a Manzanita-lined valley leading down to the Pacific, got out our instruments, and commenced to play.

Well, you could not overlook Tony's guitar pickin'.

I had never heard a steel-string acoustic guitar played so hard and hot. Tony whipped the rhythm. He *was* the rhythm, and his rhythm was ferocious, even as he stood stock-still and ramrod straight.

When I looked closer at his right hand, I realized I'd never seen this kind of flat-picking by an acoustic guitarist. His right hand was doing something jazz guitarist Howard Roberts called the "spin-drive" method. Tee held the pick between the upper side of his curled-in index finger and his thumb, like most folks. But most folks flatpick just from the wrist and forearm. Tee moved his thumb, flatpick and index finger as a unit. Squiggling this unit around furiously, like writing with pen on paper, Tee got all over the guitar, popping the strings with his tortoise shell pick.

Another thing: Tony's right wrist seemed arched out more than most folks'. He didn't anchor his wrist on the guitar. It was away from the instrument, putting weight behind an attack when Tee went full bore. Don't get me wrong; Tony was only loud when the music called for it. He had full dynamic control, from whisper to shout.

Playing with Tony was playing along with Tony, following him; rhythmically, he propelled the tune. His rhythms, interwoven, urgent, and precipitous, were far beyond the limits of bluegrass guitar as I had ever heard it. He finished his chorus with a flurry of right hand thrashing that left me breathless.

It was beyond commenting on. I stood there at the end of the tune, not knowing what to do. There was some shuffling of feet, some clearing of throats. I finally muttered something about the sanctity of poop.

Tee was awesome; he had rewritten bluegrass guitar.

Because Tony picks harder than anyone in the known universe — it must be physically wearing to play the guitar as hard as Tee does — his tone is unique.

So, Tee's first lesson on guitar is, "Attack the note."

Tee attacks the note.

He jumps on it. He lashes out at it. He rips it. He whips it. No one attacks the notes like Tee.

His furious attack makes the guitar sing out, pushes the instrument to its vibrational limits. In this I believe Tony brings sounds out of the flat-top Martin that have never been made before. He wails on chorded tone clusters, making the interval dissonances ring out so loudly against each other that the guitar roars with the clash of notes, overtones and difference tones, the clicking of the pick on the strings, and the slapping of the strings on the frets and the fingerboard.

One evening we had a gig at the Bear's Lair at U.C. Berkeley. Tony was standing to the side of the small stage, guitar strapped on, about to light a cigarette.

He held it to his mouth with his left hand, in the "V" of his middle and index fingers. He had the lighter *and* his flatpick in his right hand.

At this moment, as he was about to light up, I said, "Tee, hit me a G, will ya?"

There was a heartbeat as Tony set it. Then, without looking, Tee flicked his right hand down at the guitar and popped a G-note as clean and clear as I've ever heard played.

The note filled the room.

Then he raised his right hand and lit the stick.

What amazed me about this is what it says about Tee's relationship to his guitar. Here he was in non-playing mode, in lighting-a-cigarette mode. But he knew exactly where that guitar was and where the G-string was, and exactly how to move his body to hit that note hard and clean, without looking down. Tee was in a constant and intimate relationship with the guitar, no matter what he was doing.

It was also at this gig that I pulled a clumsy move. Tee's

Martin was lying on the floor, stage right. I picked up my bass, high, and moved it from one side of stage right to the other.

Understand that a bass is about as big as a person, a bulky, pear-shaped person. Over the years, you learn how to pick this person up, move him, put him down. After a while you think you know how to move your bass without touching it to anything, ... ever.

Well, I thought wrong. I picked up the bass, and as I floated it over Tee's Martin, I heard a tap. I didn't feel a hit — the bass has so much momentum — but I heard a tap. I looked down; I didn't see a blemish. But Tony had seen the transaction go down. He walked over, looked, and showed me the blem that my bass's endpin had just put in the finish on the top of his guitar, ... that *I* had just put on his guitar.

I was mortified.

It wasn't a ding; I didn't ding the instrument, I don't think, or I'd like not to think. It was a blem the size of a dime, on the finish of an already well-worn guitar. But I was heartbroken, and I apologized sincerely.

I recall that the bassist Buell Neidlinger was over at my digs one day. He accidently put a blem on my century-old Czech bass. He was aghast at his move — no one wants to injure another man's fine stringed instrument.

Buell said this immediately: "I apologize. I always try to move an instrument carefully. I will pay for whatever damage I have done."

He had done no damage that warranted repair. The next time my bass went in for its periodic restoration, a six-month odyssey that takes place once a decade or so, this blem and all other blems were sanded away and refinished.

But his response was complete: I always try. I sometimes blow it. And I pay up when I do blow it.

So Tee, I apologize. I blew it. And if there was a bill, please send it on over.

. . .

In the spring of 1977, Tony and I drove down to Santa Cruz to pick up the first Tony Rice Model guitar from the Santa Cruz Guitar Company, run by Richard Hoover and Bruce Ross. The instrument was loosely based on the 1935 her-ringbone Martin D-28 that pioneering flatpicker, Clarence White, and then Tony, owned.

That D-28's most distinguishing feature was the oversize sound hole — the circular hole in the middle of the guitar's top. Clarence had enlarged this O-hole on his Martin, I guess, to "let more sound out." The SCGC Tony Rice Model had that enlarged sound hole as well. And another thing: there's a pellet gunshot hole in the Clarence White Martin, some-where below the 18th or 19th fret, that was not replicated in the SCGC guitar. Legend has it that Clarence put it there late one night.

When we got back to Tee's home in Kentfield, Tony started playing the new guitar right away. And right away he heard something wrong.

"It don't sound right. It don't feel right," he kept saying. "Something's off."

It sounded right to me.

Then he'd be playing it and he'd reach to fret some first fret notes with his left hand, and he'd say, "Something's the matter, the notes ain't there."

They sounded there to me.

So he took out a yardstick and measured the string length from nut to bridge on the Clarence White Martin, and then he measured it on the Tony Rice model. The string length was 1/8th inch longer on the Santa Cruz than on the Martin. Tony could feel the 1/8th inch and the string tension that it added. He could hear the tonal difference.

That's when I knew that Tony had ears for days, and the guitar was a part of him. The folks at Santa Cruz made the changes Tee wanted, and kept some of their own modifications and innovations. The SCGC Tony Rice Model is, I understand, their bestselling guitar.

Tony's famous Clarence White Martin was not being played for a spell, and there's a story behind that.

I visited Tee and his wife Pam in Florida, in the winter of 1991. He picked me up at the Tampa airport late one evening. We drove in the dark to their house in Crystal River, in the southern part of the state, on the gulf coast. Tony told me he lived right on the water, but when we pulled in I couldn't see a darned thing. They put me up in the guest bedroom. I was pooped from a day of flying and logged off instantly.

The next morning I was awakened by the sound of a diesel engine right outside the window, maybe fifteen feet away. I thought, OK, there's a trucker got his rig parked next door in the driveway. He'll pull out soon enough.

Sure enough, after he had warmed up, he did pull out, only it was not towards the highway. Near as I could tell, it was towards the water. Well, it was early, I was still dazed, … so who knows. I went back to sleep.

Two hours later I got up, Pam gave me a cup of coffee, and Tee took me around outside. We went out the living room door to a gently downward-sloping lawn. Twenty feet out, at the edge of the lawn, was a five-foot drop to water and Tony's runabout.

We walked to the rear of the house, and it was on the water too, maybe ten feet from the bay. Then I looked around to the back of the house, the side where I had been sleeping, where the trucker had his rig parked. It was on the water too, fifteen feet away. It wasn't a diesel truck that had been parked there; it was an industrial tow boat. It was just pulling back in as we walked around.

Tee's house was on a small peninsula, a slim rise rimmed by water on three and a half sides. Only the driveway connected it to land. At that moment of low tide the water-line was maybe fifteen feet below the floor level of Tony's one-story house. As we got into Tee's runabout to jam out to the Gulf of Mexico — Tee could only drive at full-throttle, or pick at full throttle — I turned to him and asked, "Aren't you concerned about flooding here?"

Tony said, "No way, Wild Bill. It would take a once-in-a-century flood to come up to the house."

Within two years, on March 13, 1993, the once-in-a-century flood hit. It was the combination of a tropical storm with a lunar high tide. At around five in the morning the fire department came around to Tony's neighborhood and ordered everyone to evacuate: no belongings, no nothin'. You get out *now*. Tee and Pamela split immediately, empty-handed except for their dog Pokie.

Three hours later, Tony paid sixty dollars to a guy in a motorboat to go over to his house and fish out the Martin. The man said the water in the living room was neck-high when he went in. He found the guitar after a few minutes, right where Tony had said it would be. It was floating face up in the water.

Tee says he got some advice from the Martin Guitar folks in Nazareth, Pennsylvania. They volunteered their services, but finally Tee called the Cincinnati luthier, Harry Sparks. Harry came to Florida and advised Tee on how to dry the instrument out, get it back into playing condition. Tony said it was two years before the dreadnought started sounding like it used to.

Tony has the Clarence White Martin back home in North Carolina now. He's playing it, taking it on the road.

I'm glad you're with that instrument again, Tee. You two share a soul.

And I'd love to have a look at it some time, Tony. I'm hoping that ol' blem I own got washed away.

BUELL NEIDLINGER

ANON

I Love the Bass

whooouuuUUUHuuMMMmmmz

There is a secret that bass players know, and we don't talk about it, because talking about it, … well, talking about it might only dilute it. So you won't hear me jaw-boning about the bass much, because I love the bass.

The string bass is a beautiful instrument to behold. I see the way little kids look at a string bass for the first time — drop-jawed, wide-eyed — and I remember how it looked to me the first time I saw one at Pete Carbone's shop: awesomely massive, overwhelmingly large, dark-toned, mysterious, powerful.

The string bass *is* a mighty instrument.

Hundreds of pounds of pressure force the strings into the bridge and onto the top of the instrument. So a string bass must be strong as steel.

But a string bass must also be supple. It must flex in the breeze, a loose-limbed, bouncing-bellied ol' boy, resonant of the low and slow vibrations.

There are essentially only two ways to carve a string bass that is both strong and supple.

The first way is to build a bass with a thin top — the top is the sounding board of the instrument — so it will be limber in its youth, for ten to fifty years let's say. After that, the thin top can't take the pressure of the strings, and starts slowly caving in.

The other method is to build the bass with a thicker top, unlimber in its youth. Then you play that bass and wait a long time. Play it and wait until the bass opens up like a well-aged wine.

Wait … a hundred years or more.

Buell Neidlinger, one of my bass teachers, told me something about this, about the age of a string bass.

But first let me tell you about Buell.

When he was very young, Buell was a prodigy on the cello. His playing was so distinguished that the music patroness, Elizabeth Sprague Coolidge, loaned him a Guarneri cello to play while he was still a teenager. And some say that a Guarnerius is as good as, or even better than, a Stradivarius.

When Buell moved over to the string bass at age fourteen, he proved equally talented. By his early twenties he was playing with Coleman Hawkins, Zoot Sims, and with jazz pianist Cecil Taylor in Cecil's classic, Greenwich Village years.

In the '60s he played with the Boston Symphony Orchestra. So Buell plays both sides of the fence. Symphony players call them the "legit" side and the "commercial" side (ouch). There are very few folks who can do that with authority.

I caught up with Buell in the 1970s, when he was living in Los Angeles. He was playing string bass in the L.A. recording scene on sound tracks and music albums. Buell was the guy they called when the bowed bass was needed. I heard that he played bass on the Maurice Jarré soundtrack for the movie, *Behold a Pale Horse,* standing next to Ray Brown, the great jazz bassist. Ray played all the *pizzicato*, or plucked, parts, and Buell played all the *arco*, or bowed, parts.

His bass sound is awesomely sonorous with the bow and

pizzicato as well. Buell can *pizz* a note on the bass, and the note will grow in volume, actually become louder for the first moments of its sounding, ... and then start to fade.

It's ear-inspiring.

When I came to him for my first lesson on *pizzicato*, Buell said, "So, you want to learn how to *pizz* the bass? Oh, there are so many ways to *pizz* the bass."

What followed was a tour-de-force demonstration of right-hand *pizzicato* techniques, from jazz and classical through one-, two-, and three-fingered *pizz*'ing, to something he called "Polish *pizz*," which produces a bell-like sound that only Buell can demonstrate.

What Buell can do with the bow is even more ear-bending. He has total control of the nuanced stroking of the bass with the bow. The bass takes a lot of energy to get vibrating. But it also requires as much finesse as playing a violin. Buell has mastered this athletic duality.

Deep, smooth, visceral sounds bloom from his bass. Buell is an artist with the bow. All in the Los Angeles music bidness acknowledge his *arco* greatness.

This is what Buell told me about the age of a string bass. He was bowing his William Forster bass, an instrument which dates from the 1700s and, it is said, was possibly played in the premier of Handel's *Messiah*. Buell remarked:

"It's gotten to the point where I don't want to play a bass anymore unless it's around 300 years old."

Well, I liked that, because until then I don't think I had ever seen a 300 year-old bass. OK, maybe in pictures, or at the symphony through opera glasses.

But touched one, ... played one? Probably not.

This gave me a new view of Buell, of the depth of his experience.

So, as I was saying, I love the bass. Because when I hold my favorite bass in my arms and between my legs and I pop that

E-string and the bass whooouuuUUUHuuMMMmmmzs a buzz deep into my gut, and my body shudders in a wave, and my stomach and chest and arms and hands are blasted by a sound tsunami, the lowest expression of all music, the *cajones,* the mocha almond fudge knee-deep-in-the-deep-muddy, beat-beating ruler of the groove and bottom of it all, … well, let me say, it feels incredible.

So I want to encourage all of you who have never played the bass, to go out tomorrow, buy yourself a string bass and start pickin' it.

You'll love it. You'll discover what the word "thrill" means.

And then of course, you'll be in on the secret.

BILL KEITH'S BICENTENNIAL BLUEGRASS BAND
SACRE COEUR, PARIS

BY PATRICK CIOCCA

TONY RICE, BILL AMATNEEK, BILL KEITH, DAVID GRISMAN, DAROL ANGER

Paris Remembers

We drove through the Normandy region of France in June of 1984. This was the very month that France was joyously celebrating the fortieth anniversary of her Allied liberation from the Nazis.

I've loved France since I first visited there as a teenager, and I've always had a mysterious attraction to this period of her history. So I was delighted that we arrived at a number of her towns and cities as their celebrations were just heating up. Each had suffered a unique war experience, and each remembered with a fitting commemoration.

What was unique about the occupation of Paris, was how viciously the Nazis treated the Parisian citizenry. If someone from the French underground were to assassinate a German soldier on the streets of Paris, the Nazis would gather around that point immediately, round up the next dozen Parisians they found — men, women, young, old, it didn't matter — line them up against a wall, and mow them down.

So it is their very *moment* of liberation from this gruesome occupation that Parisians deliriously commemorate.

The week we were there the French government projected period documentaries on blank building walls throughout Paris. They all showed footage of the American troops — us Yanks — marching into The City in 1944 while the Parisians mobbed them, threw flowers at them, threw themselves at them, in joy and thanks.

But for us Yanks, in 1984, Paris had forgotten.

We were shortchanged and treated rudely, many times. This Parisian chill is well-known to American tourists; it seems to come with the wine.

.   .   .

Tony Rice was the guitarist in our ensemble which was officially named the Bicentennial Bluegrass Band. But Tony dubbed it the "Keith Unit," after our leader, the brilliant banjoist, Bill Keith. Bill created a style of melodic banjo-picking so distinctive that it is named after him: "Keith Picking." Darol Anger played fiddle, David Grisman, mandolin, and myself, string bass.

Tony of course picked the flat-top guitar; that is, he played his 1934 Herringbone Martin D-28 with a flatpick or plectrum. These days most flatpicks are made of celluloid. At their cheapest, music stores buy them by the gross, stamp them with their logos, and give them away to their customers.

But Tony used tortoiseshell picks. The French call them "*des vraies médiators en écaille*," true shell picks, and they are the choice of discerning flat-pickers who love the unique tone they produce and who can afford them.

Tortoiseshell picks are made from the shell of the Hawksbill turtle, which is an endangered species. The sale of "tortoise" is banned in most countries and the world supply has dried up as prices have spiraled. Tortoise fans actively seek out what is left of the world stash. It's an underground matter and sales are usually cash.

We dogged tortoise wherever we toured. In Paris we asked all our friends and local musicians for leads. One of them suggested that a certain gypsy band at a local carnival had good possibilities.

It was a traveling carnival and it took us two days to catch up with them at a flea market in a working class suburb. The band was led by a genuine-looking, walleyed, oud player. (An oud is an Arabian lute.)

Sure enough, he used a flatpick: a rhinestone-encrusted, orange dayglow plastic job, stamped with a "Paris Musique" logo.

The guitarist, who sported a Jimmy Hendrix knee bandana and a three-day old shave, used white, oversized, plastic picks which he hand-cut from tourist credit cards. He swore to me that he pick-pocketed them for that purpose alone.

The day following this disappointment, a French friend, Mary-Paul, directed us to an address in a shabby, residential *arrondissement*. There was no sign on the street indicating a music store might be down the small alley. We barely squeezed inside the place. In the cool dark it had the smell of horsehide glue, varnish, and rosin dust.

The *propriétaire*, a gentlemen in his late 60s, hurried to turn on the light for us. The bare bulb revealed over twenty mandolins, lutes, and guitars lining the walls, most of pre-war vintage. The mandolins, the speciality of the shop, were all of the Italian, bowl-backed shape. "Tater bugs," we call them down South, for the way they look.

This joint was authentic. Bill Keith and I were our French-speaking spokesmen:

"*Monsieur, s'il vous plaît. Avez-vous des vraies médiators en écailles?*" I was so pleased I had taken French in high school.

"*Non. Absolument pas!*"

Well, we all understood that.

But behind him was a wall of small wooden drawers, and on the end of each he'd pasted the item that was inside. At least a dozen drawers had variously-colored plastic picks, but we noticed that two of them had plectra that were definitely tortoise.

"*Monsieur, s'il vous plaît. Qu'est-ce que vous avez là?*" Bill asked, pointing at the two drawers.

"Oh yes. Those are true shell picks, but not for you," he said, but in French, of course.

Not for us! "*Pourquoi?*" Bill asked. How come?

"They are all too soft for your needs," was the gist of his response.

If he was right, the gentleman had a good point. Tony has encyclopedic knowledge of tortoiseshell picks, and one day he gave us a talk on the subject as we drove to a gig in Keith's orange Mercedes minibus.

Tee told us that tortoiseshell picks are made from an organic substance, so each one has a different feel. The feel of the pick comes from the quality of the shell it is cut from, and the size and thickness of cut. A plectrum may be too thin or soft for an individual player, as the gentleman was suggesting, or too large or firm. A good tortoiseshell pick should be evenly brown to dark brown, without any ripples, pie-baldness, or light-colored veins which show where the pick will break if it is stressed.

And here Tony pulled a tortoiseshell pick from his pocket, bent it on a yellow vein which ran through it, and snapped it easily.

So you don't buy tortoiseshell picks by the gross. You audition them by hand, one at a time.

"May we take a look at them anyway?" I asked the gentleman.

"*Mais certainement!*" he replied.

With a flourish he whipped out the two drawers and presented them to us at the counter.

We all gasped.

It was the largest stash of tortoise I have seen in my natural life. We were looking at hundreds of glistening, solid-brown plectra, worth thousands. Many of them *were* too soft for our needs, but many were going to be just right.

The auditioning process began while Keith and I chatted with the old man, a mandolinist himself. He seemed interested to hear we were a touring string group, and asked where we had been performing. Bill told him about the festivals we had played in Gerte, Courville, and at Nyon, on beautiful Lake Geneva.

Then I asked him how much he wanted for the picks.

"You choose which ones you want, count them up, and I will make you a price. But first, tell me one thing. What country are you from?"

As soon as I translated this question, Tony turned to me and said: "Bill, you tellum w'ur 'Muricans!"

As the old man heard this, a facial tic rippled his cheek. I was sure the price had just tripled for the rich 'Muricans and gave up hope on the project.

I took a walk, bought a half-dozen postcards, found a neighborhood bistro and wrote home over a sandwich and a beer. Then I found a post office, bought some stamps, mailed the cards and returned to the shop.

They were still sorting out picks.

Finally, they had chosen a hundred plectra. They were fully, gleefully prepared to plunk down what amounted to their tour wages in exchange for this find.

A moment of truth had arrived. I turned to the old man:

"*Quel est le prix, monsieur?*" I asked him what the price was.

"*Combien d'écailles avez-vous?*" He wanted to know how many picks we had.

"*Cent*," I said. A hundred.

He paused. "*Pour vous . . .?* " For you?

"Oui, monsieur," for us.

He looked right at me. "*Pour vous ... 'Muricans?*"

"For you Americans?" he wanted to know.

Now I could hear it coming. This was going to be one million Francs, two cartons of no-filter Marlboros, and three pair of Levi's, extra wide.

"*Oui, Monsieur,*" I answered. "*Pour nous Americans.*"

"*Pour vous 'Muricans, ... c'est gratuit.*"

My jaw dropped.

Tony looked over at me. "Bill, what did he say?"

"He said that for us Americans it's gratis; it's free!"

"Free? Well Bill, ask him why."

So I asked the gentleman, "*Et pourquoi, Monsieur?*"

And he told us. He said, "Because in 1944, you 'Muricans, ... you liberated Paris. And you never charged us a *sou.*"

Some Paris-bound pickers found their way to the gentleman's shop a few years back. They asked him if he had any tortoiseshell picks.

He said, "I sold them to some crazy 'Muricans some years ago. I have a few left. But they are all too soft for your needs."

NRPS Logo

by Michael Ferguson and Kelley

New Rider
On the Purple Sage

I'd been told that the single women who follow acoustic music groups tend to be a tad more ... cerebral ... than the women who follow rock bands. So I was pleased to receive a call one afternoon from the country rock group, New Riders of the Purple Sage, asking me to play electric bass with them on a tour of the Midwest. The New Riders were related to the Grateful Dead, so Jerry Garcia would sometimes fall by and sit in. They also attracted their share of outlaw bikers and what some folks might call groupies. I accepted their offer with delight and dusted off my Fender bass. A genuine rock tour would be a first for me.

We arrive at the sound check for our first gig and I walk on stage to set up the Fender. Out in the room, a half dozen ladies are dancing to taped music. Except for the bartender and the sound man, there isn't a guy in the house, so I figure they're here alone.

As we walk on stage, the pace of their dancing picks up and what had been freeform hippie dancing becomes more focused; they all dance facing the stage now. We haven't plugged in yet, but it's like we're already playing.

The ladies' eyes, mostly closed before we entered, are now wide open, checking us out. We act like nothing is coming down, but we're aware that we are being watched.

As Patrick, our drummer, starts his sound check, the sound man kills the taped music. The gals stop dancing and scatter to the tables and the bar. None sit together. The bar ladies don't acknowledge each other. None of them drinks alcohol; it's all Pepsies and 7-Ups. They sip their drinks slowly and watch us.

When the five of us have finished our individual sound checks, we play a tune together. This brings the ladies back on the dance floor and they boogie full tilt to our music. They come closer to the stage now and their bodies move with language that any musician can read.

We return to the club for our show that evening and go down the back alley to avoid the crowd out front. Two guys from an infamous biker gang are waiting for us outside the back door. One of them has fists like wide-screen TV's and the other looks like his big brother, only meaner.

John Dawson, our lead singer, greets them with a cheery, "Howdy guys. What's happenin' ?"

"Hey John, is Garcia going to be coming by tonight to play with you guys?" the smaller but somehow more menacing one asks.

We're in Chicago, Jerry lives two thousand miles away and just happens to be playing with the Dead this evening in San Francisco.

But John says, "Hey man, he might fall by tonight. Ya never know. But tell me somethin', where are your hogs, man? Ya got 'em parked out front?"

"Out front? Hell no. We parked 'em inside."

"Inside? The club lets you park your Harleys inside?"

"No. The club don't let us park 'em inside. We just park 'em inside." Now they rush back in to tell their friends that Garcia might be showing up that evening.

I turn to John. "Hey man. Do you always lie to guys who can kill you? I mean, telling them Jerry might fall by ..."

John shrugs it off. "They'll have forgotten by the end of the second pitcher."

Inside the club, the room is full. When our first set comes, I walk on stage, plug in, and look out at the dance floor. It's jammed with people now, and it looks like most of the sound-check ladies are back. They're still alone, but dressed, as Chuck Berry sang, in tight dresses and lipstick.

The first set is a solid two hours and the crowd pounds the floor boards. The hard-dance dimension of good rock is here. The band has pumped the room and we exit the stage to the smell of 300 sweating bodies.

During the break, most of the band head for the dressing room. But I head for the bar, post myself on the only empty stool, and order a Coke-squeeze. By the time the doctor sets it up, one of the ladies who had been at the sound check is standing next to me.

One of the nice aspects of playing out — playing out in public — is the rapport female audience members establish with guys in the band. They've seen you play on stage and they feel they know you enough to approach you and start a conversation. I like that. As a basically shy guy, I don't meet women easily. As a performing player, meeting women is simple: you just hang out.

She says, "I noticed you playing on stage. You have a nice face."

Please understand that most music fans, when they approach you after a show, will compliment the band or say something about your playing, like, "You had a good groove going, dude." The closest I've come to hearing a body part complemented was when a fan said to a fiddler, "Good left ring-finger, man; great independence." Well, string players work on freeing the ring-finger from the pinkie- and middle-finger lock, so I understood. But when a woman tells a musician, "You have a nice face," she's not making a statement about his music; I think it's a shade more personal.

"Why thank you very much. And how did you like the music?" I'm genuinely curious.

"That was nice too," she says coolly.

"My name's Bill."

"Yes I know, Bill. My name's Claire."

After the last set, Claire is hanging around the stage, so I invite her back to my motel room for a bite to eat.

It's 2 AM, I have no food, there is no room service.

She knows this, and she says, "Sure!"

As we head out, the two biker guys we met on the way in are sitting on their hogs just outside the front door, revving their engines. The bigger, meaner one says,

"Hey man, come here a second. I got somethin' I wanna say to you."

My heart stops. "Uh, ... sure man, what's up?" I am desperately trying to think up some less-than-lame excuse for Garcia's no-show at the gig.

He says, "You guys were the greatest. Boogie city, dude."

"Well thanks, man. That's very kind of you to say."

Having escaped death, and with an able-bodied woman on my arm, relief is not the word here; I feel like I'm leading a charmed, rock 'n' roll life.

Claire and I arrive at my room, I slip the Do Not Disturb sign on the door knob, and we settle in for our duet.

There comes a point in an evening such as this when it becomes understood between a man and a woman that they are going to ... to do the wild thing together. It begins after reaching the horizontal, but before clothing has disappeared. It's an interlude where people reveal things about themselves, explain themselves, to each other.

Claire says, "I'm a freshman at the University of Chicago; haven't declared a major yet. I love music and I love to dance, but I don't play an instrument. So I don't think music will be my major. Maybe English."

And then, after we've shared our first kiss, she says, "I've never done this before, ya know. I'm not a groupie or anything." She says it in an accusatory way, as though I've called her on it.

"That's good, Claire, I didn't think you were. I've never done this before either."

I'm not sure what it is I haven't done before that I'm about to do now, but it feels like the right thing to say, and Claire seems glad to hear it.

When you've gotten up at 7 AM, traveled all day in a compact car, eaten deep-fat-fried food for lunch and dinner, and then put out a large amount of sweating energy playing loud rock for four hours, sustained social activity, at 3 AM, is something that can elude you, much as you wish it would not. So our time together is not so record-breaking. I don't mention it to the guys, and I don't imagine Claire writes home about it either.

She leaves at light; we've been together maybe three hours. She has an English Literature class at 8 AM and does not want to be late.

I never learn her last name. I never hear from her again.

At seven that morning, the phone rings. It's Richie, one of our two roadies, with a wake-up call. This is another day of driving — some 300 miles due west and south — a fast-food lunch on the road, short naps in the car, a sound check at six, dinner at a greasy spoon, and the first set at nine.

When our last set is over, I go over to the bar for a soda. This time, one of our guitarists tags along.

"What's up, man?" I ask him.

"I saw that you got lucky last night. I'm just sticking with you to see if some of it rubs off on me, man."

"Sure. But I'm tellin' you, I didn't do nothing. I just sat at the bar and hung out."

"OK, Bill. I'll just sit with you and hang out too."

In a short while, two young ladies come over and ask us for our autographs. The detail of bringing pen and paper to this signing has escaped them though, so we settle on a pencil stub the bartender gives us, and two drink napkins.

I end up talking with Debbie. She is a sophomore in college, an art history major. I ask Debbie if she'd like to come with me back to my room — no pretense of food this time — and after a demure heart beat, she says Yes.

The moment of we-know-what-we're-doing-here seems to arrive sooner, as do the true confessions.

Debbie says, "I feel kinda funny being here. I want you to know I've never done this before. I'm no groupie or anything like that."

Her words are so similar to Claire's that I almost laugh out loud.

"Uh, … well, that's good, Debbie. I didn't think you were. And I want you to know I've never done this before either."

I feel badly about the white lie. Whatever it is I'm saying I haven't done before, I *have* done before, and just last night.

Debbie leaves at dawn. I don't get her last name, and I never hear from her again.

By the third night, the entire band — David, Patrick, John, Buddy, Allen, and the roadies, Richie and Bernie — follows me to the bar after the second set.

"We're sticking with you, Bill; you've got the touch," one of them says.

"I'm telling you guys, I don't do anything. I just park my-self on the stool and wait."

"Yeah, Bill. Whatever you say. But our buddy here got lucky last night and he *never* does."

So the eight of us are sitting at the bar, eight big guys hogging one end of the bar. If the bar were a boat, it would be sinking. The room is emptying, there are no females in sight, and I figure my chances are from zip to zero.

But no, eight ladies who had been sitting at a table around the corner from the bar, incredibly, like out of a movie, come over and start chatting. It feels like boy-girl heaven. For a moment I consider switching to electric bass permanently.

One of them sidles over to me. "Hi, my name's Patty," she says. "I really enjoyed your playing, Bill. You've got great hands."

Another body parts person, I imagine.

But here she takes my left hand and spreads it out on the bar, palm down, fingers splayed. She plants one of her hands by my thumb and the other by my pinkie. Then Patty holds her hands up in front of us, maintaining the length of my hand's span between her hands.

She smiles broadly. "Not bad, Bill. Not bad at all!"

We burst out laughing.

"What's this all about?" I ask her.

"I'm a nurse."

"A nurse?"

"Well, a student nurse. And in nursing school they taught us that there's a strong correlation between the size of a man's hand and the size of his ..."

She never finishes the sentence.

I believe that as we've driven southwest, deeper into the American heartland, the women have gotten faster. This is the most forward gal I have ever met. We turn and walk to my motel room, no questions asked.

The small talk isn't small, it's nonexistent. But when it

comes to true confessions, I decide to take the lead:

"I want you to know I'm kind of new at this, Patty. I'm no rock star or anything. I've never done this before."

"That's OK," she says. "I'm kind of a groupie. I love music. And I just *adore* musicians."

JERRY GARCIA - APRIL 28, 1974

BY JON SIEVERT

Jerry Loved to Pick

I got a call one afternoon from mandolinist David Grisman, someone I've enjoyed picking with many times over the years. It seems that David had spotted a rare old banjo — this was a pre-World War II, gold-plated, Weyman 5-string banjo — and he had brought it home for his old friend, Jerry Garcia. Jerry, of course, was the leader of the Grateful Dead and a rock guitarist. But originally Garcia was a bluegrass banjo picker, and his very first instrument was a Weyman 5-string that he no longer owned.

The moment Jerry laid eyes on this Weyman, he fell in love with it. He strapped it on, picked a few notes, turned to David and said, "Call up a bass player. Let's do some bluegrass pickin'!"

So, David was calling me that afternoon to see if I could come over *now* to pick some bluegrass with him and Jerry Garcia.

Well, ... I had heard of Jerry Garcia.

So, I cancelled the rest of my life, tossed the bass in the back of the car, and was over at David's before he had hung up on our phone call.

.　.　.

I walk into the living room, and there, larger than life, is Jerry Garcia. First thing I notice about Jerry is, he's got a wall-to-wall smile that lights up the room. It sits behind a massive salt-and-pepper beard and a mane of salt-and-pepper hair.

He's wearing a plain black T-shirt — no Grateful Dead logo — plain Levi's, plain black high-tops. He's got this gorgeous Weyman strapped around him.

We reach out to shake hands and I say, "Hi, my name's Bill."

He says, "Hi man, I'm Jerry."

Well, ... I know that.

Jerry starts showing me the Weyman. He points out the mother-of-pearl inlaying on the fingerboard, the engraving on the gold hoop. He flips it over and shows me the wavy grain of the pearwood resonator. He *loves* this banjo.

At this moment, David finally hangs up on our phone call and strolls into the living room. He gets out his Martin guitar, I unpack my bass, Jerry's got the Weyman strapped on, and we decide on the bluegrass classic, "Roll in My Sweet Baby's Arms."

Garcia kicks off the tune on the banjo. As soon as he starts playing, his face lights up into an even bigger smile, and I see this about him:

That Jerry is living the hippie vision of the '60s, which is, after all, the vision of love.

That Jerry gives his love through playing music.

And that Jerry *loves* to pick.

Then Garcia sings the first verse.

Ain't gonna work on the railroad.

Jerry never did, not in any sense.

Ain't gonna work on the farm.

That neither.

Gonna lay around the shack,
Til the mail train comes back,
And roll in my sweet baby's arms.

Now that, I guess, Jerry did. Then David and I harmonize on the chorus:

Roll in my sweet baby's arms,
Roll in my sweet baby's arms,
Lay around the shack,
Til the mail train comes back,
And roll in my sweet baby's arms.

Above the clucking of the banjo, the boom of the Dreadnought and the heartbeat of the bass, I hear a familiar voice singing plaintively. It is a voice that in its own way is as recognizable as Sinatra's. It is Jerry Garcia's voice — an American classic.

It was around this time that Jerry was helping out on an album by the bluegrass guitarist and singer, Red Allen. Garcia had played banjo and guitar on a couple tracks.

The next time I bumped into Jerry was on April 5, 1993. By then the album had already done well for Red. It was the first recording Allen had ever made that had recouped its expenses and gone on to pay him royalties, most likely due to Jerry's appearance on some of the tracks.

I ran into Jerry as he was walking out of the 7-11 on Miller Avenue in Mill Valley. He had a soda in one hand and two packs of cigarettes in the other.

I had to tell Garcia that Red Allen had passed away just two days before.

"What did he die of?" Jerry asked me.

"Well, Jerry, Red had been a longtime cigarette smoker. He, uh, ... he died of lung cancer."

Jerry looked down sheepishly at the two packs of cigarettes he was holding. Then he looked up at me and said, "All the old-timers are goin'."

The last time I ran into Jerry was at San Francisco's Davies Symphony Hall, back in the greenroom. This was following a concert by the grand master of jazz violin, Stephane Grapelli.

Stephane has since passed on. But in his day, Grapelli, it has been said, was the most-recorded jazz musician in the world. His tone on the violin has never been surpassed. If there is a song that the word "gossamer" sings, it is of the lightness of Stephane Grapelli's violin playing.

Well, Stephane was in the greenroom receiving company. I had already gone through the line and congratulated him on a magnificent show. At this moment Grapelli was sitting on the sofa, chatting with none other than Isaac Stern, when ...

In walks David with Jerry Garcia. David brings Jerry over to Stephane Grapelli and introduces these two music giants by saying:

"Stephane, I'd like you to meet an old friend of mine. This is Jerry Garcia."

Stephane smiles, says "*Enchanté!*" reaches up, and shakes Jerry's hand. But clearly there is no recognition on his face as to who Jerry Garcia might be.

David sees this, so he continues, slightly louder, "Jerry is the leader of the rock group, the Grateful Dead."

Stephane replies, "*Ah oui. Mais certainement!*" though again you can see in his face that he has no idea who Jerry Garcia *or* the Dead might be.

But Grapelli senses that he is being introduced to *someone* important, and that he should say *something*. So Stephane Grapelli, who is eighty-four years old, looks up at Jerry Garcia and blurts out:

"Myself, I am just grateful to be alive!"

STEVE MARTIN CRACKS WISE
JOHN MCEUEN AND JERRY GARCIA CRACK UP
GOLDEN STATE BLUEGRASS FESTIVAL, APRIL 28, 1974

BY JON SIEVERT

ALI AKBAR KHAN
BAY AREA GRAMMY AWARDS, SAN FRANCISCO, FEBRUARY 15, 1998

Swimming the Oceans

Steve Gorn, an old college friend, was visiting me in Mill Valley. We had played in a band together at Penn State, modestly called the Jazz Spokesmen. Steve led the group, composed for it, and played sax and silver flute. After he graduated, Steve fell in love with the bansuri flute and moved to India to study the instrument and immerse himself in the culture.

He was staying at my home that week while on a North California tour. One of his concerts was at the Ali Akbar College of Music in Kentfield. The college was founded by Ali Akbar Khan — Khansahib, he is called — who is a master of the Indian sarode, a 25-string, un-fretted, plucked instrument. Khansahib's playing drills down to the center of my being, and it was the renowned violinist Yehudi Menuhin who called him, "possibly the greatest musician in the world."

I drove Steve to the concert at the college, a blissful evening of Indian classical music. Afterward, while Steve was relaxing in the greenroom, Khansahib phoned and invited Steve over to his home for a reception. Since I was driving, I got to tag along.

I'd had a standoff with my dad on the phone that day, so as we drove we started talking about fathers and sons. I asked Steve how he had related to his father, a professional pianist who had passed away four years before.

"My father was not supportive of my jazz saxophone playing," Steve said. "He had called it 'primitive.' And as to my Indian flute playing, he simply couldn't hear it.

"But when he died, I wanted to honor his life. With the help of some of his old cronies, I held a memorial service at home and invited a hundred of my father's friends and relatives. The plan was for anyone who felt the spirit to stand up and say something about my father.

"I spoke first, and when I was halfway through I made a casual, maybe slightly sarcastic remark about my dad's non-support of my music.

"Immediately a friend of my father's stood up and said, 'You're wrong Steve. Your father was very proud of your music. He always told me when you had a record coming out or when you were playing a big concert. Once we were together in a restaurant, the radio started played your Indian music ... and your father went wild. He stopped everyone who passed our booth and said: "Ya hear that? That's my boy Steve playing!" ' "

Steve turned to me and said, "I felt this was a message to me from my father. Maybe he had been listening all along."

We drove in silence, and then Steve continued, "But have you heard about the relationship Khansahib had with *his* dad?"

Steve told me that Ali Akbar Khan learned his music from his father, Baba Allauddin Khan, who was revered in his time as an *acharya,* a master, the most knowledgeable person in his field. As a boy, Khansahib would awaken, dress in the dark, and put in a four-hour practice session before breakfast. Then he'd take a long lesson from his father, a second practice, lunch and a quick nap. A third practice session followed, and finally a lesson from his father that went deep into the night.

Ali Akbar Khan followed this eighteen-hour a day regimen, within the environment of a formal Indian court, until he left home to marry. Then he took lessons from his father every time he visited home, until Khansahib was fifty and his father was in his hundreds.

That's a lot of instructional time with dad in any man's culture, and it made me wonder about the relationship of this famous father and famous son — what it must have been like.

Khansahib's cottage looked warm and homey as Steve and I pulled up. His number one American student, James Pomerantz, opened the door. Behind him were Ali Akbar's wife, Mary Khan, and then Khansahib himself. We removed our shoes and they led us through the house to a dimly lit sitting room. Various religious symbols lined the walls: there were Buddhas, crosses and altars, pictures of Hindu and Moslem saints.

Khansahib asked us about drinks, and since he was drinking Scotch, Steve and I went for the same. We took seats in a circle and Jim brought us the round. Steve had first met Khansahib twenty years ago, so they had much to talk about.

But finally there was a lull. Though I was sitting across from Ali Akbar in the circle, the circle was small. I leaned forward, put my elbows to my knees, and I was *this* close to his face. Even then I couldn't read his age, he was so vital, so I said to him: "Khansahib, may I ask, how old are you?"

"I am sixty-nine."

"And what religion are you?"

Mary and Jim laughed. Khansahib smiled and gestured to the display of assorted religious icons: "I'm all religions, as you may see."

"Khansahib, you have had a long and productive career. At age sixty-nine, what are your music goals?"

Jim asked Mary, "What did he say!"

"He asked him what his music goals are," Mary replied.

"This I want to hear!"

Khansahib said, "Oh yes. I have definite music goals. I want to swim the oceans of the world. I want to swim in all the music oceans."

"What kind of music is your favorite?"

"Oh, Indian music, most certainly, and Western classical music, Bach and Beethoven. But to me, Indian classical music has heart. So much music I hear, like this rock and roll, has no heart."

We all smiled at that.

"Khansahib," I said, "you have learned a lot of music in your life."

"Yes."

"Much of that music you learned from your father."

"Yes. I learned much from my father."

"Over a long period of time."

"Yes, a very long time. And after my father died, I continued receiving music lessons from him."

"Then could you please tell me this, Khansahib: All his life the son hears the father telling him what to do. After a while the son wants to say, 'OK Dad. Enough already. I heard it!' And yet you had to take instruction from your father as both a son *and* a music student for a very long time. Please tell me this, Khansahib, how did you deal with that?"

Khansahib's dark-brown eyes lit up. The master sat up tall in his chair and he grinned widely with the wisdom I sought. *This* question he was going to enjoy answering.

"That's easy!" Khansahib said. "I hated my father. Yes, I learned much music from him. But I hated my father ... sometimes.

"I hated … that he *made* me practice. I practiced so much, I had no chance to play. So I was *fifty* before I started *loving* music.

"When I started loving music, I started loving my father."

STEVE GORN
THE 6ᵀᴴ & B GARDEN, NEW YORK CITY, JUNE, 2002

BY HALLIE LAKSHMI GOODMAN

KATE WOLF
COURTESY OF HANNAH AND MAX WOLF

ANON

A Maker of Songs

Nothing ruffled her serenity except the slow arrival of a recording session. Then she would get a little catch in her throat, a cough that she'd try to wash down with herbal tea. But it was just prerecording jitters, nothing unusual.

Other than that catch, Kate Wolf struck me as the most serene person I'd ever met. She was a Northern California singer-songwriter, and I had the pleasure of meeting Kate, getting to know her some, and playing on a couple of her albums in the late 1970s and early '80s.

Songwriters such as Kate are always asked, "Which comes first, the music or the lyrics?" With Kate, as far as I can tell, writing the lyric came first; then she'd compose the music. Spoken or recited, her lyrics sounded like poetry to me, and to me she always seemed to be a poet.

Her images are vivid. Her lyrics ride on the rhythm and lope on the line. Her rhymes tweak the ear, making her lyrics easy to remember. Folksinger Tom Paxton said, "With

Kate, the message was always — always — love." Yes, Kate, both as a lyricist and as a human being, was always about love.

She called one afternoon in 1981 and said, "Bill, I have a lyric that needs music. Would you like to collaborate with me?" I said Of course, and she came over to my digs in Mill Valley. Kate said she was looking for a country sound. Then she read me her poem.

> Gray-haired and flint-eyed,
> His sunburned face lined,
> Grandpa was a man of few words.
> He had a way of not wanting to say,
> Any more than he thought could be heard.

> The long years of living
> And day-to-day giving
> Had carved a map on his face.
> With little to lose, he'd learned how to choose,
> And his choices were easy to trace.

Then the chorus came in:

> He had the eyes of a painter,
> The heart of a maker of songs, a maker of songs.
> And his words fell like rain
> On the dry desert plain,
> Precious and so quickly gone.

A tune crept up on me. It was in waltz time, with what I thought was a progressive country feel. The melody of the verse was fairly simple, and the progression was expressed with the basic I, IV, and V chords of American roots music. Together, I felt they let the verses' lyrics be heard clearly.

The music of the chorus was a dollop more complex and

pushed the traditional country envelope. One of the chords was a half-diminished seventh chord — a minor seventh chord with a flatted 5th — something you don't hear all that often in country music. It added torque to the line, "And his words fell like rain," and twisted an otherwise fairly straightforward chord progression. To me, it was the pivotal chord in the music. The next stanzas read:

From a long line of teachers,
And white Baptist preachers,
He was born with an Indian will.
His quiet dark eyes, reading the light
As he rode in the low Osage hills.

His school was the prairie, the sage, the wild berry,
The quail, the wide open sky,
The cottonwood thicket by the slow rolling river,
The Redbud and the hot cattle drive.

He had the eyes of a painter,
The heart of a maker of songs, a maker of songs.
And his words fell like rain
On the dry desert plain,
Precious and so quickly gone.

She told me that the lyric was about her ex-husband's father. "Grandpa," as the song called him, lived in Hogshooter, Oklahoma, and was the son of Baptist teachers and preachers on one side and Cherokees on the other. He had blue, deep-blue eyes. Electric, she said.

Kate had an insight into him one afternoon. They were sitting in his kitchen, talking. She was about to go out for a ride, so she asked him what to watch for. He said that she should watch the light. That was when she knew he had the eyes of a painter.

There were days filled with thinking,
Nights with the drinking
For a lost love that raged like a storm.
But how his eyes smiled, when he'd talk to a child,
The rough hands so gentle and warm.

His strong arms were brown,
where the long sleeves rolled down,
On his faded blue cotton shirt.
When times got hard, he'd go out in the yard,
And cuss away some of his hurt.

He had the eyes of a painter,
The heart of a maker of songs, a maker of songs.
And his words fell like rain
On the dry desert plain,
Precious and so quickly gone.

Kate called a week later to explain that the ex-husband, about whose father the song had been written, was himself a guitarist. But he couldn't play the half-diminished seventh chord. She wanted to know if I would change it.

I was surprised that she was asking for a change based on ... *on the ex's not being able to play a chord!* The chord is easy to make, actually feels good in the left hand once you learn how to grab it. I told her I'd get back to her. But while I was licking my wounds, figuring out what to do next, Kate sat down and wrote her own music for the lyric.

An old friend, composer Gary Malkin, told me I had done wrong: "Always give the client what she wants," he said. Gary was right. But I'm happy that in the end it helped Kate come up with her own music. The song has been one of her audiences' favorites.

I didn't see Kate much past 1982. We talked on the phone once or twice, but her career was changing. She was on the road more, recording, writing, meeting new folks. Then, in the spring of 1986, she was diagnosed with leukemia. Within eight months it had called her home. She was forty-four when she died on December 10, 1986.

I remember how Kate could touch an audience. They loved what I loved: her centered calm, her beaming heart. She made them feel they were all in a living room and she was talking with them. She was accessible; she was adored.

It was more than her presence that won an audience; she wrote honestly beautiful songs that singers record to this day, that still touch people. There's an annual folk music festival at a ranch in Laytonville held in her honor: the Kate Wolf Memorial Music Festival. It draws a bigger crowd every year. Her spirit continues to influence even more of us.

I learned much from Kate and have more to learn from her. All who knew her or were touched by her music miss her love.

Now the garden's grown dusty,
The hand axe lies rusty,
The door's banging hard in the wind.
Grandpa's store is closed down, like most of the town,
And it won't be open again.

And the big white car, sits out in the yard
Of the house he built solid and true.
But I see his eyes, burning tonight,
Like the stars in the sky he once knew.

He had the eyes of a painter,
The heart of a maker of songs, a maker of songs.
And his words fell like rain
On the dry desert plain,
Precious and so quickly gone.

PIPER BILL MILLIN
RANVILLE, FRANCE, JUNE 6, 1994

Brotherhood of the Stick

There is a period of history that has mysteriously called me since I was a kid, ... the liberation of France from the Nazis, a saga that finally began with the Allied invasion of the Normandy beaches on June 6, 1944. I went to Normandy for the fortieth and fiftieth anniversaries of D-Day, Debarkation Day. The fortieth was a wave of quieter ceremonies that rippled through the Norman countryside, riding in the wake of the original invasion front.

The fiftieth anniversary saw tens of thousands of vets from America, France, England, Scotland, Australia, Canada, and New Zealand, travelling through Normandy in vintage army jeeps, ambulances and trucks that they had brought over at personal expense. It was likely the world's largest block party.

On that fiftieth anniversary of D-Day, June 6, 1994, I was staying at the Normandy farmhouse of an old friend, Jean-Francois. I knew that the landing beaches of Omaha, Utah, and Juneau would be jammed with world dignitaries, their guards, and the French police. So I headed off to one of the only other French towns that would be celebrating its liberation that day, Ranville.

Ranville was a vital crossroad for Germany. The reinforcements she sent from Calais to her front line in Normandy all passed through this hamlet. So it was the first French city the Allies liberated on June 6, at just past midnight. In an attack spearheaded by three Horsa gliders on neighboring Pegasus Bridge, the 2nd Battalion, Oxfordshire and Buckinghamshire Light Infantry, and the Royal Engineers, under the command of Major John Howard, retook the town.

Fifty years later, the veterans of Ranville returned to remember. I joined them to commemorate what some in the American press had been calling the last "good" war.

I parked my car on the outskirts of the hamlet — Ranville's population is about fifteen hundred — and started out for the war cemetery by the church, three country blocks away. I caught up with a veteran who introduced himself as John Hammond. I asked him what he had been doing on D-Day.

"I parachuted with the 6th Air Landing Brigade close by to Pegasus Bridge. The first commander with his three gliders, at about six minutes past midnight on June the 6th, landed at Pegasus Bridge. His three glider pilots were magnificent in the execution of the job. They dropped those gliders so close to the bridge that the soldiers in the gliders were able to take that bridge in *six minutes*. They cleared the explosives in *fifteen minutes*.

"They had to hold that bridge until the seaborne forces came in," Hammond said. "The first to arrive was Lord Lovat with his commandos, and they marched right across the bridge with their piper Bill Millin. It was a simply *magnificent* sight."

John Hammond had imaged it more vividly than the movie *The Longest Day*. In that film, Peter Lawford played the English aristocrat, Brigadier Lord Lovat, who, with his 6th

Commandoes of the 1st Special Service Brigade, landed on Sword Beach at 8:40 AM. Lord Lovat's personal bagpiper, Private Bill Millin (played by Millin in the film) marched up and down Sword beach skirling Scottish airs — "Highland Laddie," and "Road to the Isles" were among them — to rally the troops. Newspapers around the world ran a photo of him trudging down the beach, playing the pipes under a dark hail of German shells. The sheer bollocks of the man walking the beach in a bloody kilt and skirling the pipes while mortars exploded around him, was an inspiration to all soldiers who witnessed it. It also earned him the nickname, "The Mad Piper."

When the Brigade trooped inland and reached Pegasus Bridge, Lovat and Millin marched bolt upright across the bridge under withering German fire while Millin played "Blue Bonnets Over the Border," a Scottish war song from the valiant but failed Jacobite uprising of 1689.

Bill Millin's skirling at Sword Beach and Pegasus Bridge, though neither the first nor last time music was used to rally troops to battle, may rank as the most fearless pickin' by any picker under fire in any war. The words of "Blue Bonnets" are sometimes attributed to Sir Walter Scott.

Many a banner spread
Flutters above your head,
Many a crest that is
Famous in story,
Mount and make ready then,
Sons of the mountain glen,
Fight for your King and the
Old Scottish border.

March, march, Ettrick and Tevotdale,
Why my lads dinnaye march forward in order?
March, march Eskdale and Liddesdale,
All the blue bonnets are over the border.

Trumpets are sounding,
War steeds are bounding,
Stand to your guns and
March in good order.
England shall many a day
Speak of the bloody fray,
When the blue bonnets came
Over the border.

I asked Hammond, "Is this the first time you've been back to Normandy?"

"No. I've been back three times, and the reason is this:

"I had a comrade, Charlie. We enlisted together; we were together for four years. He looked after me; I looked after him. Now when we were on leave, prior to the invasion, he had a bad feeling.

"And he said to my father, 'Pop, I don't think I'm gonna make it this time. I don't think I'm coming back.'

"As a young man of twenty-four, a bit facetious I guess, I wouldn't accept what he was saying. And I said, 'Well if you're going to stay there, I'll come back and see you, Charlie.' And low and behold he didn't come back. He lies in Ranville church yard. And ... "

Here John Hammond cleared his throat; his eyes glassed.

"So I had to come back. I've come back a third time, and this time I went to his grave and I said, 'Charlie, I'm not coming back again. I'm getting too old, Charlie.' So that's why today I can go home in the knowledge that I've kept a promise; it's a nice feeling I'll have for the rest of my life."

"Has the world learned anything from World War II?" I asked him.

"No, no. The politicians haven't learned a bloody thing. They're as daft as ever. They still get us into wars, from World War II to Viet Nam to Bosnia. There's just no stoppin' the politicians from waging war. They're bloody cockups."

. . .

Hammond left to join the official ceremony in the Ranville War Cemetery at the town's center, which was closed to the general public. I stood on top of a mill wheel propped up against a stone tower, with a dandy overview of the cemetery, the church which dominated it, and the town.

Vets and young soldiers, wives and widows of veterans, artillery freaks, history buffs, French locals, and tourists — a large crowd of Yanks, Frogs, Brits, Jocks, Aussies, Kiwis, and Canucks — were all gathering. We were high-spirited and very much connected to a Normandy-wide feeling of excitement and anticipation on this historic day.

As the ceremony approached, the place jammed up with easily 10,000 people. Tourists started passing me their cameras to take shots of the action. The star of the show, England's Princess Margaret, arrived in a police convoy and took her place near the cross-topped obelisk at the center of the cemetery. I heard the buglers blow and the brass band trumpet, but when the Princess said her say, the sound system couldn't carry it; I didn't catch a word. In twenty minutes she had been swept away in the police convoy, and the official ceremony was over.

Then the unofficial ceremonies began.

The veterans and their guests went across the road to a large hall where the town was hosting them to a champagne reception, an art at which the French are well versed.

I walked in, tossed back a bubbly, and found two veterans who were two drinks ahead of me, a good sign of openness to conversation, I've always thought. One of them, a Scotsman I reckoned, introduced himself as Alec.

I asked him, "When you were down there fighting on D-Day and afterwards, what were you fighting for, Alec?"

"I was fighting for the stick, man!" He seemed genuinely surprised by my question. "Everyone there was fighting for the stick."

"The stick? Alec, what's the stick?"

"Your jump buddies; the mates who jumped with you from the plane."

"And how many in a stick, Alec?"

"Oh well, that depends, doesn't it? Sometimes ten will be

PEGASUS BRIDGE, JUNE 6, 1994

in your stick, sometimes twenty."

"You mean you weren't fighting for democracy or for freedom or ... "

"Don't be *daft* lad, *no* one fights for that. No one. Yer fightin' to save yer ... " and here he pointed to his backside, "and

BENOUVILLE, FRANCE

your mates'. It's the brotherhood of the stick, lad."

I asked Alec and his friend if they had seen best friends fall.

"Yes. But there's nothing you can do about it. Ya don't even stop to kiss 'em good-bye. Ya just keep on moving forward towards your objective."

"Did you ever have to kill a man face to face?" I asked.

Alec's friend turned on his heel and walked away.

Alec said, "Maybe we had to, yes. But that's nothing we'll be wantin' to talk about," and he walked off too.

On the way back from my next trip to the bar, I found myself standing next to two young, blue-beret'd British paratroopers. They were two of twelve-hundred paratroopers and veterans who had parachuted over Ranville the day before, June 5th, which had been designated "Airborne Day." They were about twenty-one, fit, and cocky with youth and drink.

"Did you guys get to talk with any of these veterans yet?" I asked them.

"These blokes here? Of course we have. We parachuted with them yesterday."

By calling them "blokes" he had said much about his feelings and respect for his elder comrades-in-arms.

"Well, let me ask you this then, and I hope you don't mind my asking, but tell me this if you would. Who is the better man: these veterans, or you men?"

One of them came back after a beat: "I'd have to say they're the better man, really: they've jumped into battle. I mean, we've read about it, we've studied it, we've practiced it, but we've never actually jumped into battle. They've jumped into battle, and that makes them the better man."

I thought it was big of him to have said this in response to my question.

"Tell me something then," I continued. "I know what these vets say they were fighting for. But what do they teach you in class that you're fighting for? For democracy ... freedom?"

"Listen to him talk," the other scoffed. "It's the stick, man."

"The brotherhood of the stick," the first one echoed. "And anyone who tells you no is a son of a liar."

They had a large laugh at my expense and headed off towards the party at Pegasus Bridge.

The cemetery was back across the street, and I went there when the grounds had been opened to the public. It was row on row of 2,563 white headstones marking the places of soldiers, most of them between sixteen and twenty-six years old when they died.

A company from a British battalion came in to have its own ceremony. There were a dozen vets, some with wives, some war widows, maybe twenty seniors in all. They had brought their chaplain with them, as well as a bugler and a young captain, the battalion's current commander.

The captain and two of the veterans took two battalion flags wrapped in gold braid from their leather cases and began assembling them. The captain gently reminded the older men of each step.

They threaded the brass ends of the two-piece maple flagpoles together. Then they hooked the flags to the poles and unfurled them with great care. They pulled on white leather gauntlets. Each man strapped on a white leather flag holster and mounted the flagpole in the leather cup. They pointed the flagpoles to mid-sky and stood at attention, their wrists faced away, elbows out. The young captain stood rigidly; the veterans stood slouched by time, but still as rocks.

The chaplain gave a blessing and then he said:

"Today we wish to thank Thomas Joseph Adcock from Oxfordshire, England.

"The elders of the town can still remember you when you were a boy, Thomas, riding like the wind down the streets in your new red tricycle and them callin' after you, 'Slow down Tommy, slow down, you'll be hurtin' yourself.'

"They remember how you married your school sweetheart,

Iris, who's here with us today. She says Hello to you, Thomas, and says how much she still loves you and misses you, and how your two daughters, Katelin and Anna, both infants when you went to war, now grown women with grown children

A DOZEN VETS, SOME WIVES AND WAR WIDOWS

of their own, love and miss their dad so, though they hardly ever knew you, lad. The whole town remembers you today Thomas, and joins with us here in thanking you with all our hearts.

THE STONE TOWER AND MILL WHEEL, SEEN FROM THE OBELISK

"Tommy, ... you died so we could be here today. Thank you, Tommy, so very much."

And we who were there in deed because Tommy had died for us, we whispered, "Thank you, Tommy."

For each of the battalion's war-dead who lay beneath our feet, the chaplain told a story which brought the man to life in front of us. In this he had a gift.

Then the bugler blew "To the Color" as the bearers began a flag ceremony that I had never witnessed. Each tucked the foot of the flagpole under his right arm and held the flag pointed to mid-sky. Then the soldiers slowly lowered the tips of the flagpoles. Then they dropped the points another notch, and then another. The lowest corner of the flags touched the ground.

I'd never seen a flag touching the ground, and I flinched to watch it happen.

They lowered the flags again and draped them over the ground, half-displayed on the grass. One more dip and the flags were fully revealed on the grass, each flagpole's point slicing the earth.

The chaplain read the names, the widows wept. Some of the vets teared up, though most had had their cries by then. The flag bearers stood like boulders and the flags lay on the grass, their colors drooped to the earth.

Each senior there had lost a comrade, friend or husband who lay buried beneath us. Their sadness flowed from them, through the flag bearers and the flags, into the earth below us, hallowing it.

For fifty years these veterans had kept the brotherhood of the stick alive in their hearts and thoughts; they had stuck with their comrades, living and dead. This was the last fight they would fight for the stick.

The tableau of these brave souls, grey stalks huddled beside white headstones under a darkening day, is in my memory. I am grateful to have been there.

DROOPING THE COLORS

. . .

Back at the hall the crowd had thinned. Most had headed for the festivities at Pegasus Bridge, and Alec was looking at his watch. There was one last question I wanted to ask him.

"Alec, there are some people in America who call World War II the last 'good' war, . . . you know, 'Good' versus 'Evil' and all that. What do you say to that, Alec?"

Here he turned on me angrily, literally whirled around on me and said:

"Bloody hell, man, World War II was no' a good war! No wars are good wars, and *no* one knows *that* like a *vet*. World War II was a necessary war; we *had* to drive the Nazis out of Europe. But World War II was no' a good war.

"You'll be rememberin' that now, won't ya lad?"

Bill Millin piped the lament at Lord Lovat's funeral in 1995. In 2001 he presented the bagpipes he had played at Sword and Pegasus to the National War Museum of Scotland in Edinburgh. Millin is seventy-nine years old and lives, a legend alive, in Devon, on the English coast.

BILL MONROE, BERRYVILLE, VIRGINIA, 1965

BY MARSHALL FREEDLAND

Big Mon

Bill Monroe was the founding father of that richly American music called Bluegrass. It was on September 16 and 17, 1946, that Bill brought his band, the Blue Grass Boys, into the Columbia recording studios. They cut ten tunes that created and defined this music.

The recordings featured Monroe's furious mandolin playing — lightning fast, up the neck — and his high tenor singing that broke easily and often into a muscled falsetto.

They featured the monstrous playing of banjoist Earl Scruggs, a machine-gun style of 3-fingered, 5-string banjo-picking that he first recorded with Monroe, and which is named after him: "Scruggs Picking." Earl's banjo-picking was bell-clear, driving, and essential. Your band may have Tony Rice on guitar, Mark O'Connor and Vasser Clements on twin fiddles, Jerry Douglas on a 1932 National-Dobro, Edgar Meyer on bass, and Sam Bush with Frank Wakefield on sequentially-numbered, Lloyd Loar-signed, Gibson F-5 mandolins, ... but without someone pickin' some kind of Scruggs-style banjo, well sir, you just ain't got a bluegrass band.

These 1946 recordings featured the voice and guitar of Lester Flatt, including his "Lester Flatt G-run," a guitar lick which figures in about every bluegrass song subsequently recorded. Lester's guitar was urgent and goading. His lead singing varnished the sound of his duets with Monroe; Flatt created the template for smooth bluegrass tenor singing that is still used.

Chubby Wise complemented the band on fiddle, adding a sawing, bluesy sound that fiddlers to this day try to copy. Howard Watts, whose stage name was Cedric Rainwater, played string bass (and sang bass and baritone). He drove the frantic 2-beat instrumentals with passion, and plucked 4-to-the-bar on tunes you'd expect to be 2-beat, irresistibly lifting the band from underneath.

These recordings were a quantum leap past whatever had been done previously in hillbilly music. This seminal band jumped from the tracks fully formed and laid down the law for all bluegrass groups to come: acoustic string instruments flogged to their limits, breakneck tempos, screaming solos, high lonesome harmonies, a galloping rhythm section wheelhossed by a honking string bass, a dollop of 4-part rural gospel, and many exceeding-the-speed-limit instrumentals. Essential American music.

Bill Monroe crossed over Jordan, as pickers say, on September 10, 1996, at the age of eighty-six. His last performance with the Blue Grass Boys was on March 15, 1996, at the Grand Ole Opry ... the Friday Night Opry. It is not often we witness the passing of a bona fide music genre creator, and it reminds me of how young Bluegrass is, fifty years young almost to the day of Bill's passing. Bluegrass has progressed since 1946, allowed more influences, and sharpened vocals and instrumental techniques, while still maintaining deep allegiance to the ancient tones recorded in '46. The course that Bluegrass takes, now that its father is gone, will be interesting to follow.

Besides these considerable music accomplishments, Bill Monroe was known as a man of few words.

I was playing behind Peter Rowan at the 1995 Wintergrass Festival in Tacoma, Washington. Peter had played with Bill Monroe's Blue Grass Boys in the 1960s, and his duet singing with the master was renowned for being tight as jaws. It was Saturday night; we were on the main stage. Peter was playing guitar and singing with his brothers Lorin and Chris. The incomparable Jerry Douglas was on dobro, and myself, string bass. Peter had just started introducing the second tune of the set when the audience burst into applause. If you've seen him perform, you know Pete is a natural storyteller. His introduction to his tune "Panama Red" is a fantasy tale that sets the audience howling every time he tells it. But this particular introduction at this particular moment in time was not *that* spectacular in my opinion.

So I looked around to see why the room might be going nuts, and there was Bill Monroe, leaning on his walking cane, trooping out to join us. Bill was eighty-four at the time, and his face showed those years. But the light inside him burned as hot as any youngster's.

When Bill arrived at the center stage microphone, he and Peter, who was in his fifties, did a mock pushing match for the mike. With a Zen-placed elbow, Monroe about launched Rowan clean off the stage. When Peter got back to a side mike, he turned to the crowd and said, "That man's got strong *chi*," which Bill did.

Then the two sang a tune they're both identified with, "Walls of Time," as lonesome a bluegrass song as there is. Bill sang an angel part so high above Peter's lead, it was ghostly. Finally they rendered a song that Bill wrote called "The Little Girl and the Dreadful Snake."

There is a old story about Monroe and this song that over the years may have become ... enhanced ... by what is called the "folk process." The folk process is about the changes that a story or song goes through as it passes orally from one person to another. So like I said, this legend may well have changed over the years, but this is the way I remember it.

At a university folk music festival some years back, there was a round-table discussion. The topic of this dialogue was "The Lyrics of Bill Monroe's 'The Little Girl and the Dreadful Snake'." On the panel were two Ph.D.'s in Psychology — a Freudian and a Jungian — a professor of American folk musicology, and Bill Monroe. The Jungian Psychiatrist, Dr. Zleitag, kicked off the symposium by reciting the lyrics, which he had transcribed from an old Monroe recording:

Our darling wandered far away,
While she was out at play.
Lost in the woods she couldn't hear a sound.
She was our darling girl,
The sweetest thing in all the world.
We searched for her but she couldn't be found.

I heard the screams of our little girl far away,
"Hurry daddy, there's an awful dreadful snake."
I ran as fast as I could,
Through the dark and weary woods,
But I reached our darling girl too late.

Oh I began to sigh,
I knew that soon she'd have to die,
For the snake was worn and weak close by.
I held her close to my face,
She said, "Daddy, kill that snake.
It's getting dark, tell mommy good-bye."

To all parents I must say,
Don't let your children stray away.
They need your love to guide them along.
Oh God, I pray, we'll see our darling some day.
It seems we still can hear her voice around the house.

I heard the screams of our little girl far away,
"Hurry daddy, there's an awful dreadful snake."
I ran as fast as I could,
Through the dark and weary woods,
But I reached our darling girl too late.

Then the panelists — well, three of the panelists — tore into the song. The first to speak was the Freudian psychologist. Freudians are fixated on dreams and what they call "transference."

So this ol' Freud boy got to talkin', Viennese accent and all, about the girl wandering "var away. Zhust like in a dream." He related how she was "lost in der voods," where the parents "couldn't hear ein sound ... zhust like in a dream." And he spoke of the father hearing "der screams of our leetle girl var avay."

"Var away," the professor repeated, "zhust like in a dream. Mr. Monroe's entire sonk iz ein metaphor fur ein dream,"

Then he pointed to the "glassic Freudian transverence" in the last verse: "Mr. Monroe has the girl transverrink her feelinks from the father — 'daddy, kill dat snake' — to the mother — 'dell mommy goodf-by' — as she lies dieink."

This was heady stuff, and the audience murmured in profound understanding.

Then Dr. Zleitag, the Jungian, who was deeply into symbolism — aren't they all — said to the crowd:

"The little girl, ... the dreadful snake. Do we need Dr. Ruth to explain this to us?

"And the line which reads 'For the snake was worn and weak close by.' Do I need to draw you a diagram?"

The crowd tittered knowingly.

In actual fact, the lyric reads, "For the snake was *warning me* close by," and not, "For the snake was worn and weak close by."

The Jungian shrink had made a Freudian slip.

Then the folk musicologist polished this off with his analysis, contrasting this song to others by Bill:

"Most of Mr. Monroe's lyrics tell simple stories with little meaning beyond the first, literal level. 'The Little Girl and the Dreadful Snake,' on the other hand, is rife with complex layers of sub-text and symbolism unique to Mr. Monroe and this micro-ethnic genre."

The room "ah'ed" in solemn appreciation.

After well over an hour, the three Ph.D.'s had come to the end of their dissection of Monroe's song. It makes you wonder whether Ph.D. doesn't stand for "Piled high and Deep" after all. Through it all, Big Mon — that's what Bill Monroe was called — Big Mon had kept silent.

Finally, one of the professors allowed that Monroe hadn't said a word. He turned to Bill, a little embarrassed, and said, "Well, Mr. Monroe, just what did motivate you, *do you think*, to write this song?" ... as though Bill himself might not understand his own true reason.

Monroe stood up and walked over to a podium at the side of the stage.

The room went deathly quiet.

He rested his arm on the lectern, leaned into the mike, and said:

"Neighbor down the road, ... his daughter wandered off, got bit by a snake, ... up and died.

"Me? ... I thought I'd write a song about it."

And with that, Big Mon tipped his white Stetson hat to the roaring crowd, and walked off stage.

THE BEACH BLANKET BABYLON BAND
CIRCA 1979

ANON

MICHAEL ASHTON
VICTOR LA GAMBINA   CHARLIE KEAGLE
SETH EVANS   BOB ELKJER

To Steve,
With Hats Off

"Musicians are out there," a friend told me when I was nineteen. "You dress different, hang out with fast women, keep late hours, ... do all that stuff straight people don't. Musicians are not like other people." I resisted this at first. But by the time I was twenty-one, I got it.

June 15, 1995

Today, some musicians, actors, singers, and dancers gathered at San Francisco's Grace Cathedral to bury Steve Silver. Steve's show, *Beach Blanket Babylon,* has been playing since 1974, as long a run as we've had around these parts. Everyone who lives in the Bay Area and every tourist who has visited the City have most likely seen the show at least once.

Over the years, hundreds of performers have played in the ranks of "Beach Blanket," or "BBB" as it is called. I am a member of this extended family.

What is Beach Blanket Babylon?

It is outrageously-hatted performers in extreme, full-body costumes, performing fragments of show and pop tunes segued together. They dance their hats off, camp it up, and sing their tonsils out while riffing on a plot about Snow White's search for love with all the wrong faces, a gamut of culture icons from Michael Jackson through Monica Lewinsky. BBB is crammed with sly campy skits, song medleys and bits, all going by in a blur while the audience roars its eyes out.

And hats. The cast wears outlandish hats and the hats get bigger and more bizarre as the show goes on.

Finally Val Diamond, who, along with Renée Lubin, was one of the stars of the show when I played there, finales with a hat as wide as the stage is wide and tall as the stage is tall. It is a hat of the San Francisco skyline with Golden Gate Bridge, cable cars, the Trans-America Pyramid, the Bay Bridge, buses and trolleys that light up, blink, and move. A hat so large that only the magic of the theatre could possibly support it. The biggest hat on the planet.

I played bass in the Beach Blanket pit band, subbing for Seth Evans, who held the bass chair for fifteen years. I don't know how it was for Seth, but for me the bass book was tough. There were constantly changing time signatures, tempos and keys, many of them sustained for just a measure or two. I had to keep an eye on Michael, our musical director and pianist, who kept us together with exaggerated head and hand movements.

Playing in a show presents unusual cues for the pit musician. They come from the director, but also from the lead singer, a dancer, a punch line, or from a bump of the ingenue's hip. BBB was a cue a second. If I let my concentration stray or got caught up in some madness on stage, I was "off the chart" … lost.

I remember the first night I went to see BBB, in preparation for playing the show. As the performers made their entrances, I sensed something different was happening.

This was not a cast of uniformly gorgeous girls and boys. (In the American theatre, performers in the troop are either called "boys" or "girls," apt names for them both.) One of the girls filled my arms when I hugged her. One of the boys was so homely looking, I thought he was the comic and this was his "duh" look.

Something different *was* happening. Steve's people were hyper-talented: wildly uninhibited actors who turned in unfettered performances. Steve picked boys and girls for their raw energies, not just stage beauty; this is not so common in the world of American theatre.

On evenings when I played the show, I would walk from the relatively tame world of San Francisco's North Beach, into Club Fugazi, the show's home on Green Street. I'd trudge up a long flight of stairs and enter the boys' dressing room and the backstage world of Beach Blanket Babylon.

It was called the boys' dressing room, but it was also the greenroom and the costume shop, so the girls hung out there too. It was the social room for all the cast and crew.

Walking into this room was walking into Never-Never Land. Dancing ballerinas in tutus, prancing queens in leotards, all singing at the top of their lungs, strutting around the room, preening, posing, primping. Everyone rushing around — many in states of undress — acting, trilling, rapping, riffing, being cranky, brassy, bossy. Everyone psyching themselves up and hoisting their own egos, as actors must. And always a dozen attendant costume mistresses, wardrobe assistants, prop masters, stage hands, publicists, journalists, boyfriends, girlfriends, the band, stage-door Johnnies, and hangers-on, hanging on.

Bedlam.

Me, I'm just sitting in the corner of the room, shades on, trying to look as inconspicuous as a six-foot-one-inch person can who also happens to be wearing a tuxedo while some boys and girls are half-naked. I'm trying to look blasé, trying to look like, Hey, I see this stuff all the time. Gals prancing around in their bras and panties, guys down to their dance belts — like a thong, only less — girls chasing boys, boys chasing boys.

I'm a musician; I'm cool. This scene is boring.

I pick up my bass and start playing scales and arpeggios, trying not to gawk goggle-eyed at this three-ring circus exploding in front of me, impossible to out-blow, out-weird.

So we musicians, for once, at Beach Blanket Babylon, we were the squares; we were the straight guys. Steve put us in that role every night we were there. He made us see ourselves from another side, and it was a hoot.

All in Grace Cathedral learned showmanship from working in Beach Blanket. Though I only met Steve once, I learned from him by playing the show he created. I went on to the next gig knowing that,

The show IS the thing,

There are No Limits to the show, but

Nobody put on a show like Steve Silver.

STEVE SILVER

BY AL HIRSHFELD

Linger on the Halftones

I am sitting at the wheel of my station wagon, waiting on a red light deep in the crotch of the San Francisco Tenderloin, when, from the corner of my left ear, I hear,

"Hey man, spare some cash for the smashed?"

I look up at a sixty-year-old bum who's staring down at me through watery eyes. Thankfully, the doors are locked, the windows are up.

"Uh ... sorry man, I'm just a musician, broke myself, and I'm due at a big band rehearsal."

"*Big band?*" he says. "Well all right! Are big bands comin' back?"

The guy is beside himself.

"Hey man, take me wit' you?"

And he's serious!

I point to the music gear that fills my Pinto wagon to the roof, shrug my shoulders, and the moment the light turns green, I floor it. And as for the big bands coming back, ask any of the old salts I'll be playing with tonight, man. They've heard *that* one before, many times.

Now either I find a spot near the union hall on Jones Street, a half block past the bum — he's not following me, is he? — or I'll have to lug all this equipment past this gauntlet of winos and walkers who make their home the Tenderloin.

I'm not complaining, though. This is my home tonight too.

So I like to get here twenty minutes early for this 7:30 PM rehearsal. And with a little luck ...

There it is, an empty parking spot, halfway between the all-night porn theater and the wrought iron gate the musicians' union has put up in front of their double doors. Not bad so far. Now to off-load the 1938 Juzek string bass, electric Fender Jazz bass, high-wattage amplifier, and the speaker bottom, all needed for this gig and all weighing in at a hundred pounds plus.

Rudy is always here a chorus before me, but this is his band, and that is his gig. Rudy is wheeling in the last of the band's charts — the musical arrangements — and with some two hundred charts for twenty players, it takes him a few trips to unload his car.

"How ya doin', baby?" he asks me.

With Rudy, it's always "baby," instead of the usual "man" or "bro" you get from most other musicians. You might think he's forgotten your name, but he hasn't. When players in his rehearsal band meet on the street, we say "How ya doin' baby?" as a testament to him, to having played in Rudy's band together.

"I'm fine, Rudy. How you doin', baby?" I answer.

As we set up, the rest of the band start drifting into this large, fluorescent-lit rehearsal hall. The wood floors of the stage are stained with brown splotches, permanently discolored by years of trombonists and trumpeters emptying their spit valves onto the ground.

It's chewed up in places by drummers who have banged their bass drum spikes into the stage, and by bass players, I'll admit it, who have done the same with our endpins.

In the far corner of the hall, facing the wall, is a trumpet player with long salt-and-pepper hair, absorbed in his warm-up routines of scales and arpeggios. Watch this:

"Hey, Walter ... ... YO, WALT!"

See what I mean? You can't talk to Walter and you can't get a word out of him, for now. Walter is a "high note" or "screech" trumpeter; he can play an octave or two higher than most other guys in the city, clean and in tune. He is also the trumpet section leader, and maybe Walter wants to make sure he blows away everyone else in his section, which is probably what he's warming up for right now.

Standing along the back wall, that long-haired kid, never saw him here before. He looks about twenty and, man, he is sweating. His fingers are locked and he's biting down on the reed of his tenor sax so hard his tone is breaking up. The kid — they say his name is Paul — couldn't be this bad or the regular wouldn't have called him in to sub.

But here comes Poppa, the leader and senior member of the sax section, who would fall off his chair if he played any more relaxed. He walks over to Paul and starts sharing some of his good-ol'-days stories with him:

"Did you realize," he asks Paul, as he loosens the sax strap around the young man's neck, "that in the first two weeks of October, 1945, twenty name big bands folded, *never* to be heard again! Twenty big bands, man; the end of the era!

"Now son, just bring your elbows in, ... that's it, and relax your jaw. You got the death grip on the reed, man. You're gonna be the end of *its* era."

By the time Poppa goes to warm up his own horn, Paul's tone has mellowed, and fatter notes shaped by looser fingers slide out the bell of his tenor sax.

There are now five trombones, five trumpets, five saxes, bass, guitar, and drums, all warming up, each oblivious to the sounds of the others, each concentrated on his own sound.

Limbering lips, flexing fingers, stretching arms: a free form jazz cacophony of rips and riffs that stops just as it is climaxing.

Rudy steps to the podium and calls out the number of the first tune for the evening, "One hundred eight-seven, gentlemen."

"One eighty-seven? You're going for the chestnuts tonight, Rudy, the *old* chestnuts."

It is the silent Walter, the high-note player, warmed up and back in his groove as band commentator.

"Just something to get the band warmed up, Walter," Rudy replies.

"Gentlemen, would you take a look at letter 'C' please. We are going to play through that section twice. Got that? Letter 'C' twice. And watch out for the *ritardando* at the end. Those last three *fermatas* will be conducted, so eyes up front. Got it?"

From the back of the hall, we all hear: "*Eh Rudy, commo se dice 'Ritardando' ?*"

It's Wally, our pianist, making his entrance ... *followed by the bum who panhandled me, two steps behind him!*

Rudy tosses off a "How ya doin', baby?" in their direction. And Wally, *and then the bum*, toss off a "How-ya-doin'-baby" right back at him!

I don't believe it! Does Wally know this guy? Does Rudy? The sight of the impeccably dressed Wally — custom shirt, silk tie, Italian shoes — with this ... this *bum* walking behind him, boggles my eyes. But the guy just sits down at the side of the hall as Wally strides over to the grand piano.

There at the keyboard, Wally instinctively knows what to do and what not to do. Wally would never double my bass part, for example, with his left hand, even if it were written in. This is something that less experienced big band pianists have not always figured out.

He arrives relaxed, precisely at 7:35, knowing that most

of the band won't be there until then, and that the hit — the downbeat to the first tune — won't be given until a few minutes later anyway.

Wally sets up his microphone and amplifier, pulls number 187 from the stack of piano parts, scans it for key signature, time signature, tempo, modulations, flow, solo sections, and tricky passages, and looks up just as Rudy counts off:

"Two bars for free. Saxes in on the pickup. Ready?
"One...Two...One, two, three, four..."

Twenty romantics, my friends, in love, hopelessly in love, with the shout of the American big band, that rare and gangly eagle, flier of flights high and wide, taker of outrageous and sentimental journeys.

Listen to the saxes tonight, soulfully moaning their smears, billowing a path through the evening air.

A soaring trumpet section, blade-sharp, and a little slaphappy with their "doites" and pops.

The trombones, like a vocal quintet, lush and shimmering.

Hot rhythm section tonight. We are smokin'!

And every soloist who steps forward this evening is ... a poet on the spot.

Sitting and playing bass in the middle of a band like this, I move in a changing relationship to time and sound. Music rushes in and saturates my ears with sound; my being is overtaken by sound. Music is all over me and around me, immersing me in an ocean of sound.

The rhythm takes over my breathing, my heartbeat clicks into the tempo. I am engulfed by music, washed away in a sound ocean.

Now I am not playing music; music is playing me. It billows over me, losing me.

I feel am somewhere else, set free of this moment.

I drift in silence, outside time, high above silk clouds.

.   .   .

The tune ends, but the bum continues popping his fingers and shuffling his step, reminding us he is still here. Some of the boys detect a kindred spirit in him and I admit he seems to be a fellow lover of music.

When we take our nine o'clock break he starts to make his way towards the bandstand, looking somehow at home in this old music room.

Now that he is walking towards the rhythm section corner — my corner — I see there is an aura of fleas that surrounds him and an aroma which precedes him by a few feet; he's slept in these clothes for months. I point him towards the heater just past the drums, but he waves me off; this is not his desire.

He shuffles to the piano, sits down, and respectfully wipes his street hands on greasy slacks.

After a long hesitation, he leans over the keyboard, puts his fingers to the keys, and to my amazement, eases into a slow, stride rendition of "Georgia on My Mind." It is rusty ... atrophied ... lopsided ... but played with small flourishes that sing quietly of past skills.

Walter leads us in giving the bum a big hand when he finishes.

This startles him, and he sits up straight to play "Moonglow" for us. His technique becomes more fluid and his memory improves as the years he gave to the piano struggle back to his fingers through an eighty-proof brain.

But in this short moment — listen carefully please — we are privileged to hear the rekindling of a talent that had nearly died.

As usual, the second set, with Wally back at the keyboard, goes better than the first. The boys have limbered up by now, and during the break many have ... consulted ... with the muse. Some have purchased a beer at the corner market. For others it is some kind of smoking, done, out of respect for nonsmokers, in the men's room, the only men's room anywhere with no graffiti on the walls, none. Respect, they say, has something to do with that too.

So the second set is looser, and yet tighter. The ocean is even more encompassing and the band catches on quickly to the stylistic demands of the tunes Rudy calls out. Basie tunes swing hard, especially the Sam Nestico arrangements. Ellington's charts reverberate with his rich, symphonic sound. The salsa tunes are *caliente*. We spin through all these charts soulfully and finish the shouters thunderously.

At the end of each tune ... silence; it has all been said. Rudi calls the next number, we bring the charts up on our stands, he counts it off. But between tunes, ... nothing.

When the last number has been played and most of the guys have packed up and gone, my homeless friend moves over to the piano and again sits down. A few of us are there talking music, and he starts to quiz us:

"OK you men, gather 'round here. Who here thinks he knows his piano? Get this. Whose style is this?"

And he starts playing an old Bud Powell tune, "Crossin' the Channel." His playing is ragged, ... but right.

Four measures into it, Paul, the nervous young tenorist, blurts out, "Bud Powell ... got to be."

The gentleman stops in his playing, pleased and disappointed to be found out so soon. He raises his eyes from the keyboard to see who would know so quickly, and smiles to find a youthful face. "Right you are, young man, very good. Now who is this?" And he plays "How High the Moon" in the flamboyant and decorated style of Art Tatum, but paced to avoid major stumbling.

Paul waits this time, and then speaks up, "That's Tatum, the great Art Tatum ... and played real well."

"Why, thank you very much, my man. And what is your name? ... Well Paul, can you tell me who this is?" And he launches into a bounce rendition of "Somebody Stole My Gal."

We listen to the whole tune, and then Paul tells us it's Errol Garner.

Now the gentleman smiles and settles gruffly into an old ballad. He plays it thick with the smoke of cigarettes and the smell of stale liquor, and accompanies himself as he continues:

"Well Paul, let me tell you somethin' about playin' a lounge, playin' piano in a cocktail lounge. You're sittin' there playin' when in walks a beautiful girl, a lovely woman.

"Right away you start playin' her tune. Play it just for her, reach out for her, follow her with her song.

"Pretty soon, see if she don't come walkin' over to you. Maybe she sits down next to you on the bench. You turn to her, look into her eyes.

"And as you end the song, you ... linger ... on the half-tones. Draw them out ... hesitate, luxuriate. Linger and then ... the end.

"She'll love it, Paul. Just remember: linger on the half-tones."

JAZZ FUNERAL &
OFFICIAL DEDICATION OF MEMORIAL MARKER

FOR
BUDDY BOLDEN

LEGENDARY JAZZ PIONEER

FRIDAY, SEPTEMBER 6, 1996

6 P.M.

Layin' Buddy Down

I was visiting New Orleans in September of 1996, strolling the streets of the French quarter, when I saw a poster in the window of the Palm Court Jazz Cafe. The poster read:

JAZZ FUNERAL &
OFFICIAL DEDICATION OF MEMORIAL MARKER
FOR
BUDDY BOLDEN
1877 - 1931
LEGENDARY JAZZ PIONEER

The poster hadn't told me much about this Buddy Bolden. I vaguely remembered that he was an early New Orleans horn man, but beyond that, who was he? This got to me too: why, in 1996, were they giving a funeral for someone who had died in 1931, sixty-five years before? So I decided to go to this jazz funeral which was the next day, September 6, at the Delgado Community College, at 6 PM.

I arrived at quarter till, expecting maybe a hundred hard-core jazz fans. What I found was almost a thousand people, black and white together, cramming the college quadrangle, waiting to give the long-buried Buddy Bolden a N'Awlins funeral.

A New Orleans funeral procession has two parts, called lines: the first line and the second line. The mourners are the second line. The first line is the marching jazz band that leads the parade, for us, Dejan's Olympia Brass Band, led by trumpeter Milton Batiste. They were four brass players, a sax, bass drum, snare drum, a tambourinist, and someone they called the Grand Marshal.

The Grand Marshal was an African-American gentleman so strikingly tall and thin, at first I thought he was standing on stilts. He was wearing a coal-black tuxedo with a black top hat and black tux shirt. He had a rhinestone-encrusted, royal-burgundy satin sash draped around him. A thick, black leather belt wrapped around his waist two times, and three differently colored, multicolored parasols were hanging on it.

At six o'clock the Grand Marshal nods to the snare drummer, and the drummer starts playing a street beat. Then the Grand Marshal blows his whistle and the band tears into "When I Lay My Burden Down." They march out of the quadrangle and into the streets of New Orleans, the second line following them, second-lining to the music.

What is "second-lining?" Well, there's a pigeon-toed strut that's big on the hips and big on the butt. The women twirl brightly colored parasols over their heads. The men whip out handkerchiefs and wave them around, all in time to the music. That's second-lining.

Then the band starts singing:

Glory, glory hallelujah
When I lay my burden down.

King Richard Matthews, Grand Marshal

DEJAN'S OLYMPIA BRASS BAND

AND THE SECOND LINE

GERTRUDE BOLDEN TUCKER – BUDDY'S GRANDDAUGHTER

And the second line joins in:

Glory, glory Hal-le-LU-jah
When I lay my burden down.

Everywhere we go, we stop traffic. Cars pull over; folks get out to join us. People walking home with groceries in their arms put the groceries down on some neighbor's stoop and fall in. Within a quarter mile, a couple hundred more second-liners have joined us. Now we have well over a thousand people marching down the streets of New Orleans, strutting, butting, twirling, whirling, clapping, singing.

But I'm thinking, Wait a minute. Funerals are supposed to be somber, sad affairs. This is no somber affair. This is a raucous street party, two blocks long.

Finally we arrive at the Holt Cemetery, a paupers' cemetery. It's in a sorry state and a shock to everyone. Most of the graves are unmarked swells of earth. A few have two tree branches placed as a cross lying over them. We do a slow, respectful processional around the cemetery until we reach a wooden bandstand, just built, off to the side. A headstone shrouded in a black cloth stands in the middle of the platform. As we gather around, some people get on stage to speechify: Ione Elioff, president of the college; Suzanne Terrell, a New Orleans City Councilwoman; Buddy's granddaughter and great granddaughter; and, appropriately, the Mayor of New Orleans, Marc Morial.

But the most interesting speaker is an old jazz professor; he tells us all about Buddy.

Buddy was described by those who had seen him as a handsome, light-skinned Negro. He took up the cornet, a cousin to the trumpet. He was so talented with the instrument that by the time he was twenty-six, Bolden had become the first musician ever to be crowned "King" of N'Awlins. And to be called "King of New Orleans" means that you are *the* hottest horn player in town.

But King Bolden had more "firsts" than that.

You see, Buddy didn't just play the melody on his cornet.

He didn't just embellish the melody.

Buddy broke free of the melody and improvised over the tune.

And that, added to the unique feeling he gave his music,

DELGADO'S PRESIDENT, IONE ELIOFF; COUNCILWOMAN, SUZANNE TERRELL; NEW ORLEANS MAYOR, MARK H. MORIAL; BUDDY'S GRANDDAUGHTER AND GREAT GRANDDAUGHTER, GERTRUDE BOLDEN TUCKER AND RITA CAMILLE BELL

is called "jazz." So Buddy was our first jazz player, and he led the first jazz group in 1895.

Then the professor told some stories on Buddy.

One tale said it was not unusual to see Bolden walking down Perdido Street with five women on his arms. Well, he was a dapper dresser and a ladies' man.

But five women? Buddy, that was *asking* for trouble.

Another story said his cornet playing was so clear and loud, he could be heard for fourteen miles.

Fourteen miles? Well Buddy, if you could handle five women ...

There was another story about Buddy.

When he was twenty-nine years old, Buddy was playing a Labor Day parade in New Orleans. It was a hot day, the band had taken a break, and Buddy, reputedly a hard drinker, had been drinking hard. They had just started up again ... when Buddy went stark, crazy, raving mad.

The police came, took him away and threw him in front of a magistrate. The magistrate threw Buddy in the East Louisiana State Hospital at Jackson, also known as the Jackson insane asylum. And in those days — this was 1907 — when you were placed in an insane asylum, the doors of your life locked behind you.

Buddy Bolden was never heard from again.

He could not give an interview, was incapable of it, and he was never recorded. Or, another story goes, he *was* recorded, on a lone Edison wax cylinder that has never been found. Most of what we know about Buddy Bolden we learned from his contemporaries, such as Jelly Roll Morton, who outlived him.

Buddy died on November 4, 1931, at age fifty-four. Some say it was booze that drove Buddy insane; some say it was women. Jelly said Bolden blew his brains out into the cornet.

The funeral home unceremoniously threw Buddy's bones into an unmarked grave at the Holt Cemetery. Over the years as many as nine folks were buried on top of Bolden; then the cemetery's records were lost. Now they can't exactly say where Buddy's bones lie, but legend has it that he rests beneath the old Oak tree that dominates Section C of the cemetery.

"Today, September 6, 1996," the professor told us, "is Buddy's 119th birthday. It's high time we were layin' Buddy down with the N'Awlins send-off he's always deserved."

With that he lifted the shroud from the headstone and we

all crowded around to read what had been said about Buddy. On the tombstone they had engraved these words:

IN MEMORY OF
CHARLES JOSEPH "BUDDY" BOLDEN
SEPTEMBER 6, 1877 — NOVEMBER 4, 1931
IN AN UNMARKED GRAVE NEAR HERE RESTS
BUDDY BOLDEN
LEGENDARY CORNET PLAYER
NEW ORLEANS JAZZ PIONEER
AND FIRST "KING OF JAZZ"

I liked that. Someone had summed up Buddy in a dozen words. But beneath this was a one-sentence quote from Jelly Roll Morton. Jelly had recorded an old song about Buddy called the "Funky Butt Blues," and later, "Buddy Bolden's Blues." It goes about like this:

I thought I heard Buddy Bolden shout,
Open up the window, let the bad air out,
Open up the window, let the bad air out,
That's what I heard him shout.

I thought I heard Buddy Bolden say,
Funky Butt, Funky Butt, take him away,
Funky Butt, Funky Butt, take him away,
That's what I heard him say.

In the music business it is sometimes said that when you sing a song about someone, it may just mean that you love that person. So I was glad to see that a person who had known and loved Buddy, had said it about him in so few words. And what Jelly Roll Morton had said about King Buddy Bolden was engraved at the bottom of the headstone:
"He was the blowingest man since Gabriel"

EDWARD PARIS, TROMBONIST

Donald M. Marquis' exceptional biography,
In Search of Buddy Bolden: First Man of Jazz,
was published by Louisiana State University
Press in 1978. It is the full story of the King.

JAZZBEAUX
SAN FRANCISCO, CIRCA 1963
COURTESY OF PATTI COLLINS

ANON

Jazzbeaux Got There

Al "Jazzbeaux" Collins, notorious jazz personality, and creator of the Purple Grotto, his radio show that lived in its listeners' imaginations, passed away on Tuesday evening, September 30th, 1997, at his home in Mill Valley. He was seventy-eight. He was one of my teachers.

I remember Jazzbeaux from the radio. He broadcast live from a state of mind he called the *Purple Grotto*, a stalactite- and stalagmite-daggered cavern, three stories below street level, somewhere in downtown Manhattan.

He described it so well, and in so few words, that he put you there with him, into the *Purple Grotto*. He filled it with characters from his imagination. There was Harrison, the purple Tasmanian owl, who stared at you through two red eyes. I remember Scoffer, who lived in the bottomless purple pit and ate the labels off old 78s. And there was Jukes, the chameleon, who lived in a box made by Dr. Caligari, the cabinet maker. The box that Jukes lived in, Jazzbeaux called the "Jukesbox."

From his Purple Grotto, Jazzbeaux cast his purple spell. He played jazz records, and Jazzbeaux had great taste in music. Between cuts he rapped at you in '50s bop-talk about whatever pleased him: about jazz, which he loved and spoke of succinctly; or about the cut he had just played. Or he'd tell one of Steve Allen's "Bop Fables" — the Little Red Riding Hood stories Steve rewrote into hipster vernacular. Or he'd have the cats in to play live on his show. He'd have cats like Count Basie — Al's favorite jazz was big band and his favorite big band was Basie's. Cats like Louis Armstrong, Teddy Wilson, and even Art Tatum. Tatum, maybe the greatest jazz pianist who ever lived, played live on the Grotto for six months straight.

Miles Davis once called Jazzbeaux up — yeah, Jazzbeaux knew Miles — and Miles, knowing how Jazzbeaux dug a good car, asked Al to take a ride with him in his new Ferrari. Sure, Jazzbeaux went. He said it was a gas.

Al was so strong in the New York scene that MAD magazine caricatured him for a while. He was one of the few hosts of the Tonight Show, doing a stint following Steve Allen and preceding Jack Parr.

He recorded "Grimm Fairy Tales for Hip Kids." This was an album of Al reading Steve Allen's "Bop Fables," while Steve played piano. It sold 750,000 copies.

So, all the cats hung with Jazzbeaux, and Jazzbeaux was one of the cats.

A pioneer in radio, he invented the man on-the-street interview in 1949: In his version, Al would lie down flat on his back at some downtown street corner — like he was gone — and when someone came over and bent down to look at him, he would stick a mike in his face and start interviewing the guy.

Jazzbeaux invented the art of talking on air over soft background music, usually by a piano trio like Nat King Cole's.

"That made my audience feel that somethin' was going

on, somethin' was happenin' in the Grotto where I was talking," Al told me.

During his show, Jazzbeaux would take phone calls from his listeners off the air, while he was playing a cut. If he found a caller that he was having a good time with, he'd take him on-air when the cut ended. He was a master of these on-air interviews and had off-the-wall discussions with his callers. The ones who gave him the biggest laughs would become mainstays on his show for years, checking in regularly to update Al on their stuff.

Jazzbeaux was an independent. He never let management dictate a play list to him; he played what he wanted, and he did what he wanted. One evening, Count Basie came by with his entire band. They played live on the *Purple Grotto* for two-and-a-half hours straight. Jazzbeaux didn't air a single commercial the entire time. The station manager was furious, and nearly fired him the next day.

"I wouldn't have cared," Al told me. "We had a blast!"

The Purple Grotto was a magic show born in a magic era of radio. Jazzbeaux took it with him for some fifty years, from New York to San Francisco, Los Angeles, Pittsburgh and finally, back to the Bay Area. He was last on-air with the Purple Grotto at KCSM radio at the College of San Mateo on September 20th, ten days before he passed. It was prostate cancer that finally caught up with him.

Early in the spring of 1997, Al and I drove to Carmel to dig Mose Allison. Mose was playing a concert at KRML radio, the local jazz station. The station had invited Al down to be their guest at the show and were offering to put him up at a fancy inn.

Al said, "Yeah, but you've gotta put up my driver too. I don't travel without my driver, ya know."

The station said, "Driver? ... uh, no problem, Al."

Fortunately, Al asked me to be the driver.

It was a beautiful day, the sun was shining on the Pacific, the early spring flowers were in bloom, and as we drove, I asked Al about his beginnings in radio.

"I looked around and I saw what the other guys were doing and I said, 'No, I don't want to do that. That's not funny, that's not refreshing. Let's talk about something that's *fun*.'

"That's my whole philosophy. The more laughs I can get and the less serious I can get, the more I like it.

"I don't believe in settling the great questions. A lot of people want to know why we're here. I'm satisfied with just knowing that we are."

And then he said this, carefully:

"I just want to get so relaxed, so mellowed out, that no matter what happens on my show, no matter what any of my guests say or do, I will be totally in the groove with it and flow with it perfectly."

He looked out the window; the Pacific Ocean sparkled in his eyes. Then he looked back at me and said:

"And I haven't got there yet."

I was surprised to hear Al say this — he was the king of laid-back — so later when we were at the inn, I asked him, "Did I hear you right, Al, that you haven't got there yet?"

He looked over at me and said, "Yeah. Not yet."

Al was a little Buddha on his way to enlightenment. And on that September Tuesday evening, in the arms of his wife Patti, with a picture, it is said, of Count Basie hanging over the bed, Jazzbeaux got there.

Hello Al. May your message of jazz and laughs liven up the heavenly big band forever.

My Friend Al Collins
Mill Valley, circa 1995

With a Count to Four

Dear Diana and Ray,

It was the best New Year's Day party I've ever been to.
THE BEST.

There were forty old friends there whom I hadn't seen in
a dozen years or more, to say nothing of a hundred others. All of them are soulful, giving, loving, exciting, active,
creative people. Each one is playing through a bloom of
creativity, each striving in his own way to be the most
truthful artist he can, to play the best he can, do the best
he can in his expression. I heard this all night from
everyone I spoke with.

There were Jon and his wife, Shellie, and their daughter
Kendall. Kendall's thirteen now! She was less than a year
old, swaddled in her mother's arms, when I last saw her.
Shellie and Jon look ingrained with clarity about who
they are and where they have been.

Jon's got a steady gig at a bar in Pacifica, a mile from

his home. He's arranged it so he can leave his instruments there between gigs fergoshsakes; talk about ideal.

He's playing guitar now, a Strat, and singing. Jon plays guitar and drums, he sings, plays vibes like he's on fire, and plays harmonica. Plays harmonica? No, he's a harmonica playing champion. He won the grand national harmonica playing championship in America some fifteen years ago. The best harpist in America!

Pat was there with his fiancée, Anne. They look blissful together! He's in a bass ensemble that has five double basses and a percussionist. They've had works written for them by Francois Rabbath and other internationally acclaimed composers. He puts on "Bass Bashes," bass-player get-togethers where hot bassists from all over the world give workshops, hang, and play. Pat's gigging with the Marin Symphony, the San Francisco Ballet, and at "Phantom of the Opera." He's got a five-night-a-week steady, AND he puts on a summer camp for bassists as well. SO HOW ABOUT A LITTLE MORE PRODUCTIVITY, PAT! YER SLOWIN' DOWN HERE, BUD!

There was Richard, the clarinettist; I played with him in San Francisco society trad jazz and swing bands. Richard played with Dan Hicks in a band called the Charlatans in a club in Sierra City back around 1962, and this band and this club, some folks will tell you, mark THE birth of San Francisco rock, if not all American Rock, as far as San Franciscans are concerned. The Charlatans were just inducted into the Rock 'n' Roll Hall of Fame. And that is terrific. I'm very proud and happy for him. Way to go, Richard! INSCRIBED IN HISTORY. It was wonderful to see him again.

There was Benny. I used to play with him behind Denise the singer. Haven't seen him in an easy eighteen years. Didn't he look in great peak, with a son who's twenty-two, and Benny is, I think he said, fifty-four and looks maybe forty.

All the musicians looked so familiar. They all have brotherly- and sisterly-ness in my life, permanence in my life, the permanence of playing ensemble together, of understanding and feeling music together. We had all shared a bond, an attachment of souls, when we had played together, when we had gotten on stage together and the lights had gone down, and the crowd was ready to listen, the crowd was waiting to dance, the crowd was ready to rock, and the crowd was ready.

With a count to four, we pointed to a moment in time, and at that moment we abandoned it all, threw it out into breathing feeling timing flowing spirits hearts-in-air. For sharing these experiences together we are a family, and your annual party is our reunion and a gift we all cherish. Thank you, Diana and Ray.

As we walked out the front stairs of your home, I realized something about all the musicians who were at your party. Of course, how much I love them.

But also, how very tender musicians are.

Warmest regards and best wishes for a great new year,
BA

Catching Up with Mary

A short time ago, I heard that Peter, Paul & Mary were going to be playing the Concord Pavilion, about an hour's drive from where I live. So I sent Mary, through one of her agents, a manuscript of the story I had written, "MARY, ... Peter & Paul." Then I bought a ticket for the show, which was still a month away, and waited.

Finally, the big day of their big show arrives. I drive out to the Concord Pavilion, go back to the stage door and knock. Who opens the door but a big, burly guard. He's not going to let me in.

After twenty minutes of my campaigning, he relents and I scamper in.

It is a huge backstage area, a major cavern of studios, refectories, passageways, rehearsal nooks, and greenrooms. Finally I find Mary, and the two of us settle down in a small dressing room.

I say to her, "Mary, I wrote a story about the time I played bass with you guys at the Bread and Roses Festival. I tried to send it to you through your agent. Did you receive it?"

She says, "A story about playing with us? Gee, I don't know. If you had a copy of it, all I'd have to do is read the first sentence or two, and I'd know whether I had seen it. Do you have a copy with you?"

I have three copies with me.

So I take one out of my coat pocket, open it up to the title page and hand it to her. There in the middle of the page is the title:

MARY, ... Peter & Paul

Mary looks at the title. Then she looks up at me and says, "Oh, I like it already!"

About The Artists

I consider myself fortunate to have the following artists and photographers represented here. My thanks to each of them for giving their kind permission to publish their works in *Acoustic Stories*.

Al Hirshfeld - Al Hirshfeld's drawings have graced the entertainment section of the *New York Times* since 1929. Your name may be in lights on the marquee of the Shubert Theater, but you have arrived on Broadway only when Hirshfeld has drawn you for the *Times*. He draws performing artists with sometimes a few perfect lines, and sometimes many, but Hirshfeld always distills and captures them, most often better than a photograph. His style is unique, and it can be said that he created his own genre. His works are in the Smithsonian Institution, the National Portrait Gallery, the Metropolitan Museum of Art, the Museum of Modern Art, and the Lincoln Center Library, among others.

Annie Leibovitz — Annie is most likely the best-known portrait photographer in the United States. She cut her teeth working for *Rolling Stone* in the '70s where she defined rock photojournalism. When she left there, I thought, Where will she go now? The answer was: Everywhere. In the last two decades she has shot dozens of covers for *Vanity Fair,* including the beautiful portrait of the beautifully-pregnant Demi Moore. This photo of Aretha was the last she took that afternoon, as I recall. Annie asked Aretha for one final shot, walked right up to her, put the camera to her face, and took this insightful portrait.

Gene Tortora — Gene studied photo illustration at the Rochester Institute of Technology, where Minor White was among his teachers. He has done album photos for many members of the San Francisco Bay Area acoustic music family. Currently, he puts his creative energy into playing the slide resophonic guitar, AKA the dobro.

Hallie Lakshmi Goodman — Hallie has been taking photos, not for a living, but, as she told me, "for my life." Her camera travels with her constantly, resulting in an extraordinary archive of the events of our time, including photographs of downtown New York in the aftermath of September 11, 2001. Renowned New Age teachers and Indian classical musicians are frequently the subjects of her work. Her abiding love of the arts has led her to photography, jewelry making, painting, dance, and playing the Indian tamboura.

Jon Sievert — Jon wrote and published the book *Concert Photography: How to shoot and Sell Music Business Photographs*, the bible of music photography. He was staff photographer and editor for *Guitar Player Magazine*. His photos have appeared on more than 100 magazine covers, dozens

of album/CD packages, and in countless books and publi-
cations worldwide, including *Rolling Stone, Musician, People,
Acoustic Guitar, The New York Times, Entertainment Weekly,
Guitar World, Vanity Fair, Newsweek,* and *Fachblatt.* He can
be found on the World Wide Web at HumblePress.com.

Marshall Freedland — A professional banjoist and gui-
tarist, Marshall toured with the Robert DeCormier Singers
in the 1960s, joining legendary bassist Bill Lee for their
New York appearances. His photographic education began
in 1964 at Goddard College with mentor John Mahoney.
FRETS Magazine published work from Marshall's 40-year
oeuvre of bluegrass and folk masters, which includes Libba
Cotton, Mike Seeger, Brownie McGhee, Peggy Seeger and
Ewan McColl, Dave Van Ronk, Merle Travis, and Doc Watson.
Marshall lives in Miami. You can view his photos online at:
http://community.webshots.com/user/bluegrassphotos.

Michael Ferguson & Alton Kelley — These two gentlemen co-created the New Riders of the Purple Sage logo. I
was told that Michael Ferguson drew the original design
which Alton Kelley then edited and colorized.

Michael Ferguson was the pianist and a vocalist in The
Charlatans, a seminal San Francisco rock group that you
may have read about. He created (along with George Hunter)
a poster for the group's first gig at the Red Dog Saloon in
Nevada City. It is considered America's first psychedelic rock
poster, and its pivotal importance to this art form led it to
become known as the "SEED."

Alton Kelley arrived early on the Haight-Ashbury scene and
was one of the founders of the Family Dog in 1965.
He went on to create many landmark posters for the Dog
and for San Francisco rock groups, both alone and in

collaboration with Stanley Mouse. He emerged as one of the foremost artists of the psychedelic era.

Patrick Ciocca — Patrick studied the upright bass at the classical conservatory of Lausanne, and has played Europe with Bill Keith, Peter Rowan, Jim Collier, and Pierre Bensusan, among others. He has done sound design, light design, and audio engineering for dozens of acts, touring in China, Thailand, Egypt, Canada, Brasil and the USA. He is currently Technical Director of the *Octogone Theater* of Pully, Switzerland.

Ray Hunold — Ray is most likely the best-known photographer of storytellers in the American storytelling revival movement. His work has adorned storytelling CDs, festival posters and programs. Many tellers have used Ray to take their publicity shots. When I asked him what he would like me to say about him here, he replied, "I have always considered myself lucky to do what I love: make photographs."

Thomas N. Tworek — "I have been gifted with the opportunity to combine two of my favorite passions, music and photography, having done both professionally for about thirty years. My insight for photographing musicians comes from playing on stage myself. I look for that moment when the musician detaches himself from the world and becomes one with his music. I try not to use a flash while photographing a performance because it distracts the musicians, irritates the audience, and flattens the image. I prefer using ambient light with all its shadows available to lend depth to the photograph. The mystery and drama remain intact."

Acknowledgments

Many people helped me along this long journey. A big thank you to: Steve Gorn, who first alerted me to the American storytelling revival movement; Betty Hodson, creative writing teacher at the College of Marin in Kentfield. One of my editors, Betty showed me that well-written fiction is more interesting than fact;

Kathryn Wyndham, master teller, who showed me that well-told facts are more interesting than fiction;

Lynne Terry, National Public Radio Paris correspondent and Oregon Public Radio journalist, who made me see the story's big picture; and to

Ali Akbar Khan, for letting me tell his story.

A big hug to all my friends, Pete Kessler and Gail Fratar, Chuck Aronson, Jimmie and Cookie Chanteloup, Dean and Dianna Devner, Steve Glaizer, Seth and Page Evans, Pat, Kathy and David O'Connell, Jay Ginsberg, JoAnne and Dick Kowalski, Chuck Eisler, Jesse Kincaid, Tom Beeson, Bob, Stephanie and Matt Levin, Marshall Freedland, Kester Smith, Lorin, Bernadette, Chris, Peter, and Candy Rowan, Peter Scott, Bruce Dettman, Jean-Francois Mode, Jon Sturtevant, Jim and Lisa Nash, Clara Yen, Joe and Karen Armstrong, all the veterans of sssssh, the Bay Area storytelling community, and all the Penn State Folkies, with many thanks for urging me on, and for indulging my sense of humor.

Thank you to: Jim Marcolina, for pix-editing expertise;

Tom Stern for early editing suggestions;

The Bay Area Independent Publishers' Association, for showing me that independent publishing is the only way to go;

Pete Masterson, for generously sharing his infinite knowledge of book making, type setting, page layout, and book design. No one has fielded as many of my book questions or fielded them as graciously as Pete;

Dr. Bob Jenkins, for his ear-opening storytelling intensive workshop at San Jose State University, and his lesson, among many others, "Hit the mark; tell your story;"

Ruth Stotter, undiluted queen of Marin storytelling, fountain of storytelling knowledge, and wise guide;

Jay O'Callahan, one of the most focused listeners I've ever encountered, and America's Dean of storytellers, who took the time to listen;

Ed Stivender, banjo picker and wild man of storytelling, who demonstrates that the teller and the tell have no limits;

Laura McNamara, Executive Director of Arts Outreach in Solvang, California, who was the first to hire me for a storytelling festival, the *Flying Leap Storytelling Festival;*

Jeannie Patterson, longtime owner of Mill Valley's Sweetwater, for bringing me to her audience, and for her lavish praise;

Milbre Burch, storytelling *acharya*, who saw what I was up to, had the heart and selflessness to write about it eloquently, and championed my application as an Exchange Place Teller at the National Storytelling Festival in Jonesborough, Tennessee.

Susan O'Connor, Director of the National Storytelling Festival, who hired me from among hundreds of Pacific Region applicants and let the national storytelling community hear what I was doing;

The New York Pinewoods Folk Music Club and Folks on Broadway, especially Heather, Joy and David, for bringing me to their delightful festival, and for their gracious hospitality;

The Folk Song Society of Greater Washington and Lisa Null for listening to my stories and hosting me lavishly;

Angela Lloyd, who always tells me about her storytelling road;

Donald Marquis, for his late-night chats about King Bolden;

Charlie Chin, mind-bending teller (and banjo picker), for showing me storytelling from another world;

Ron Jones, his excellent wife, Deanna, and guitarist Kenny Martha, for delightful storytelling memories;

Rudy Castro, for a blissful time in his shoutin' band, Rich Bice, for the Full Faith and Credit Big Band experience, and all members of the Faultline Big Band and of Jump House, for indulging my directing;

John Weingart, Vickisa, and Gene Shay, for having me on their radio shows, and for their wise insights;

Saul Broudy for late night email advice, and to all my friends at the Philadelphia Folk Song Society, Tossi Aaron, Andy Braunfeld, David Baskin, and Esther Halprin, for their memories and for the Bob Dylan memorabilia;

Thom Etheridge, for the frank video;

Hannah and Max Wolf, Terry Fowler and Nina Gerber, for their memories of Kate Wolf;

Jim Cooke, leader of SSSSSH, the Marin County story swap group (meets at 7:17 PM on the second Sunday of each month at the Tiburon Community Congregational Church) — for my money, the best swap group in the USA — who heard and encouraged me when I had a little voice;

Kate Frankel, for her glowing warmth and encouragement;

Bruce Latimer, for having me on his television show so many times, and for his enthusiastic support;

Steve Rennick, for his eye-opening analysis of this book's layout, his insights into the cover's design, and for his sense of visual rhythm;

Susan Rabin, *chanteuse*, Dan Hicks "Groovette," songwriter, playwright and music attorney, for her sharp advice;

Jonathan Kirsch for his invaluable and insightful advice on book publishing rights;

Al Collins, who gently tried to get me to drive the Celica slower, and his wife Patti, for sharing Jazzbeaux with me;

Pete Seeger, music-with-storyteller pioneer, for his boundless spirit and long-time family friendship;

Charlie Pearson, for his deft insights into the manuscript;

Ann Chandonnet for her editing, and for making "Brotherhood" sing;

Jann Wenner of Rolling Stone for hiring me early on; and

The magazine editors who took the time to read and publish my "Acoustic Stories" even though their magazines didn't necessarily publish "stories." Thank you, Peter Kuykendall and Sharon Watts of *Bluegrass Unlimited*, Ed Enright of *Down Beat*, Stephan Bodian of *Yoga Journal*, Brian Boldt and the staff of *First Leaves*, and Jane Love of *The Dickens*.

I say a special thank you to Darrell Martin, my storytelling coach, who passed away recently. I didn't know anything about story*telling* until I met Darrell. When I first saw him perform, I realized that he was like a jazz musician who used *all* the instrument: it's timbres, range, tempi and meters. Darrell used all of his body, all of his voice, all of the stage and all of his emotions. I told him that I had a lot to learn from him, and asked him if he'd coach me. When he agreed, I asked him what he wanted in exchange. He said, "I only ask that you improve." You were a blessing, Darrell. I only hope that I have improved.

Most importantly I thank my wife Lenona, whom I love, for all her love, patience and trust. No one has heard my stories as many times as she, and that takes devotion.

PERMISSIONS

The author tried diligently to obtain the permissions and releases necessary for publication of the material in this book and for the protection of the sensibilities of the people it depicts and names. If anyone mentioned or depicted in *Acoustic Stories* is in any way embarrassed, violated, or offended by finding himself here (or by not finding himself here), the author apologies sincerely and profusely.

Many thanks to Paul Tannen for permission to use the lyrics to Bill Monroe's, "The Little Girl and the Dreadful Snake."
Used by permission, Tannen Music,
A Division Of New Media Music Inc.

A big thank you to Mitchell Greenhill for permission to quote the lyrics of:
"Your Long Journey"
By Rosa Lee Watson and Doc Watson
Copyright Hillgreen Music (BMI)
Used by permission

My thanks to Max and Hannah Wolf for permission to reprint the lyrics to Kate Wolf's "Eyes of a Painter:"

"Eyes of a Painter"
Words by Kate Wolf
Copyright 1981 Another Sundown Publishing
Used by Permission
www.katewolf.com

"Leaving On A Jet Plane"
Words and Music by John Denver
Copyright © 1967; renewed 1995 Cherry Lane Music
Publishing Company, Inc. (ASCAP)
DreamWorks Songs (ASCAP)
Worldwide Rights for DreamWorks Songs administered by
Cherry Lane Music Publishing Company, Inc.
All Rights Reserved   Used By Permission

For permission to use the photo of Aretha Franklin by Annie Leibovitz, special thanks to Annie and to Jeffrey Smith of Contact Press Images.
© 1971 Annie Leibovitz/Contact Press Images,
Courtesy of the artist.

My thanks to Margo Feiden and Nancy Mirsky for permission to reproduce Al Hirshfeld's portrait of Steve Silver:
Copyright by Al Hirshfeld. Art Reproduced by special arrangement with Hirshfeld's exclusive representative, The Margo Feiden Galleries Ltd. New York.

Thank you to Deborah Kohler, Assistant Director of Public Relations at Delgado Community College, New Orleans, Louisiana. The cover of the Buddy Bolden jazz funeral program is used by courtesy of Delgado Community College.

Many thanks to Andy Braunfeld and the Philadelphia Folksong Society for permission to reproduce the Society's flyer for Bob Dylan's May 3, 1963, concert.

For permission to reprint the NRPS logo, created by Michael Ferguson and Kelley, thank you, John Dawson.

Thanks to Ray Hunold for permission to use his photo of laughter that appears on the full title page, and to Thomas N. Tworkek, for his dynamic photo of live bluegrass.

Namaste to Hallie Lakshmi Goodman for permission to use her photo of Steve Gorn at the Garden.

Thank you, Marshall Freedland, for all the banjo you taught me during Philly Folk Workshop days, and for your iconic photo of Bill Monroe.

My sincere thanks to the anonymous photographers and artists whose works are in these pages.

Finally and importantly, my thanks to old friends Jon Sievert, Gene Tortora, and Patrick Ciocca for permission to use their photographs.

Designed and composed in Bookman
with display lines in Parisian
by Bill Amatneek for Vineyards Press, LLP

Sheetfed press offset-litho printed
on opaque stock
by McNaughton & Gunn, Inc.

Ordering Acoustic Stories

I f you'd like a copy of *Acoustic Stories* and can't find it at your favorite bookstore, you can buy it directly from the publisher, Vineyards Press, LLC.

Ordering is easy at our website, www.VineyardsPress.com.

Or photo-copy this form, fill it out, and send it to us with a check or money order.

US ORDERS: Air shipping is $4.00 for the first book, and $2.00 for each additional book. Postal media mail shipping is $2.00 per book and may take two weeks.

SALES TAX: Please add $1.20 per book for orders with California shipping addresses.

INTERNATIONAL ORDERS: Add $9.00US for the first book; add $5.00US for each additional book.

Name _____

Address _____

City, State, Zip _____

E-mail _____

Qty	Item	Price	Total
____	*Acoustic Stories*	$15.95	____
____	Shipping (see above)		____
____	Tax per Book (CA Shipments) $1.20		____
	Total Enclosed:		____

Send this information and your total remittance to:

Vineyards Press, LLC
P.O. Box 716
Sebastopol, CA 95473

You can email us at Orders@VineyardsPress.com.

Or phone us at 707.823.1492, Monday through Friday, 9AM to 5PM Pacific Time.

This offer is good until December 31, 2003, when prices may change.

THE PETER ROWAN BLUEGRASS BAND
JANUARY 18, 2003, MOUNTAIN VIEW

BY THOMAS N. TWOREK

AVRAM SIEGEL, THE AUTHOR, PETER ROWAN

About the Author

Bill Amatneek has recorded with Mark O'Connor, Kate Wolf, the Chambers Brothers, Tiny Moore and Eldin Shamblin, the Rowan Brothers, and on the first David Grisman Quintet album. He has played string bass with Frank Wakefield, Peter Rowan and Tony Rice, Bill Keith, Peter, Paul & Mary, and the Full Faith & Credit Big Band.

Rolling Stone, Down Beat, Bluegrass Unlimited, Musician, Pacific Sun, Yoga Journal, First Leaves, and *The Dickens* have all published Bill's stories and essays, and he is anthologized in the book, *Encounters with Bob Dylan.* Bill was runner-up in the William Faulkner Writing Competition of 2000, and Guest Editor of *The Men's Issue* of *Storytelling Magazine,* in March, 2001.

He tells tales from *Acoustic Stories* at folk, bluegrass and storytelling festivals, accompanying himself on bass and banjo. Bill has been seen flying with Peter Rowan and the Free Mexican Air Force, playing bass with Lorin Rowan and Kester Smith in the band Rattlebox, and directing Jump House, a twenty-piece Santa Rosa big band. He lives in Western Sonoma County.